MIND OVER NATTER

OVERCOME NEGATIVE INNER CRITICS
THROUGH EVERYDAY MINDFULNESS FOR
HEALTH, WEALTH, LOVE, AND HAPPINESS

TOVÉ KANE

Copyright © 2020 Tové Kane
All rights reserved.

978-1-64746-542-1
978-1-64746-543-8
978-1-64746-544-5

All illustrations Lisa Kane.
Except, Pencil sketch of Keegan, by Tové Kane.
Except, Peanuts with Charlie Brown and Snoopy, by Charles Monroe Schulz.

Dedication

For Lisa who knows my inner critics and loves me anyway.
I adore you, Sister Mine.

TABLE OF CONTENTS

Foreword vii

Author's note ix

Preface 3

Acknowledgments 7

Introduction—What Does Mind Over Natter mean? 11

Chapter One
Something's Wrong. Am I stuck here forever? 23

Chapter Two
Mindfulness—What Is It and Can I Learn How to
Practise It Right Now? 53

Chapter Three
Mindlessness—My Life's a Mess. What Can I Do about It? 81

Chapter Four
Look Who's Talking (and Who's Listening) 113

Chapter Five
Selfie Time—Am I Really Not Good Enough? 147

Chapter Six
Resilience—How Do I Bounce Back?. 193

Chapter Seven
Go for it! 231

About Tové Kane. 251

Bibliography. 255

FOREWORD

by Dr Madan Kataria
Author of Laughter Yoga
Founder of Laughter Yoga Clubs Worldwide

Our inner voice can sometimes be extremely cruel and judgemental, and the nagging and criticising is often unrelenting. We automatically accept that what our inner dialogue says is a true reflection of who we are! We don't yet understand that these inner voices can be challenged, or even changed, and our assumption that what they say is true is a major cause of stress in our lives. Learning to be mindful is beneficial on many levels, and importantly, allows us to "hear" the constant nattering in our heads! It also then allows us to discern whether these voices hold any truth, or do some need to be discarded.

Tové Kane's new book, *Mind Over Natter*, offers a refreshing look at how people caught in the cycle of stress and sickness, whether it's physical, emotional, or mental, can use mindfulness to gain insight into their internal dialogue. Tové explores how mindfulness helps us discern if a voice offers worthwhile advice or harmful criticism. When we are able to clearly differentiate between the harmful and helpful voices we start to heal old wounds and learn to re-direct our inner dialogue to help and not harm.

Tové has studied directly with me in Laughter Yoga and she has a wonderful way of opening hearts to new possibilities, and her heart is central to her story. It's a story of strength and resilience. She mindfully laughs through her own loss and grief and teaches from a place of compassion. Her sense of fun shines through her words.

Mindfulness is a massive subject with an enormous amount of literature, but Tové makes it accessible and the techniques easy to implement. She teaches some body-mind practices which will be useful, no matter what level you find yourself at.

Enjoy *Mind Over Natter*, and give yourself permission to play with Tové, give yourself permission to be vulnerable and use the techniques suggested in this book to calm the nattering, eliminate unnecessary stress, and gain a sense of hope that you can change what no longer serves you.

Dr Madan Kataria
Mumbai, India, July 2020

AUTHOR'S NOTE

I can't.
I'm stupid.
No matter what I do…
I'm not enough.
It doesn't matter how hard I try…

Sound familiar? I've said them thousands of times. Self-limiting beliefs, excuses, negative inner critics—call them what you like—we all have them. The names we often call ourselves are cruel and unkind. We talk ourselves into problems, and therefore, we dismiss our passions. We uphold opinions that are outdated and untrue. It's time to identify these opinions, let them go, and replace them. How about a life that's more fun and fabulous?

Many of us teeter on the brink of being overwhelmed. It's painful to feel stuck, shackled to the past, and seemingly unable to do anything about it. Living in the pain of our past blinds us to our present. I was heavily under the influence of my past, caught in a trance of tendencies, habits, sadness, resentment, guilt, regret, and a destructive self-image. It wasn't only about my body image. My whole vision of myself was distorted along with my potential, my preferences, and even my identity. I kept trying to re-create myself through dysfunctional lenses.

I spent years suffering chronic pain, fatigue, anxiety, and depression. To the world, I appeared vibrant, enthusiastic, and successful. If you've ever had to show a brave face when secretly, you were in pain, I truly get that. That's why I wrote this book for you—to show you that I identify with your struggle. If you're in two minds, that's understandable—I felt the same way. If I could heal, perhaps you can too. I'd like to believe *Mind Over Natter* can make that possible, or at the very least, start you on the path of healing. Whether you have a chronic illness (mental or physical) or are struggling with the pressures of daily living, I hope overcoming your negative inner critics will relegate your suffering into insignificance. Your efforts in mindfulness are about to bring you greater rewards than you may have ever imagined.

It's time for a new story, a new phase, a new you! Yours is a life of belonging and connection, of genuine happiness, optimal health, love, purpose and abundance. Despite the reluctance of your negative inner critics, you can change the way you respond to pain, insomnia, fatigue, low energy, suffering, stress, anxiety and depression. There's a scrumptious banquet of delights waiting for you.

Mind Over Natter is going to help you update your self-image and improve your life. We update our technology, but we don't bother updating or refreshing our view of who we are and what we want. You'll encounter resistance from your inner critics. They have a strong hold on you right now – and that's okay! I'll show you how to get beyond self-limiting beliefs to enjoy ever-expanding health, wealth, love, and happiness.

Each chapter starts with some of my original poetry which lightens as the journey lengthens. Many people have blocks against poetry, but I find it a great way of articulating and compacting meaning. The short verses will hopefully emulate your increasing ability to cope as your resilience grows. There's an essay on each theme, plus some examples and exercises which will help you implement the suggestions into your life. "Be Bright, Be Brief, Be Mindful," recaps the main points in the chapter. At the end, there's a meditation you can read, watch on YouTube, or listen to the audio.

My invitation is to read each chapter sequentially, but if you open the book and something resonates for you, that's fine too.

There's a meme that says unscramble the letters in "depression" and you'll get, "I pressed on," which is a fantastic reminder that your current situation isn't your final destination.

Fancy doing some unscrambling with me to get you moving towards your dream life?

My love and affection to you.

Enjoy the journey.

PREFACE

Land, Sea and Cityscapes of the Mind.

Self-judgement and cruel reproaches create harsh mental landscapes. Imagine a scale of landscapes from one to ten that starts with a scorched, dry surface. No wonder we feel so desolate after a lifetime of dragging ourselves across the treacherous wastelands in our mind. The irony is we aren't even aware that we have created this bleak inner world. We struggle along unaware that it is our thinking that is arid. Negative thoughts detrimentally impact our lives. Without being conscious of it, we live with a sense of doom - a defeatist, cynical, obstructive, rigid, cold, mental atmosphere that leaves us stressed and exhausted.

Advancing across the scale, you might have an inner world that is less hostile, perhaps the conditions aren't as harsh, but you can't escape the sense of isolation and loneliness. The next is not quite benign but not quite fine either. Perhaps the blandness leaves you slightly empty, moderately discontent, a malaise of mediocrity? That's not a fun place to be is it, who wants that?

Sure, you're not scolding yourself but the quiet isn't really stillness because you are screaming inside.

What about adding some water as a means of describing your mental landscape? Is it a lake? Is it flat, cold, dark? What lurks beneath the surface? Or, is it a happy, holiday lake full of colourful splashes and wonderful memories? Perhaps you could depict your mental state as a river. Is your river dry? Are there carcasses of your hopes and dreams lying exposed, fading to dust under the sun? Is your river flowing with toxic thoughts that are poisoning your life? Is it a raging torrent that demolishes people, places and opportunities around you? Sure, your outbursts may be intermittent, it's not like you're in a perpetual tirade, but the damage you inflict on yourself and others is substantial when you're in full flood. For some of us, our mental landscape feels like an ocean of overwhelm, like we are just moments away from drowning.

Moving further along the scale, does your landscape feel like a foreign land where you can't read the signs? You feel helpless, not knowing where you are or where you're supposed to go or how you're supposed to get there? Confusion exacerbates your sense of anxiety.

How about the frenzied hurry of Times Square in New York? It's noisy, distracting, hard to focus, tough to lock on to one thing since big screens loom large distracting you at first then intimidating you, almost closing in on you, replaying your regrets over and over. The giant screens depict agonizing future scenes that terrify you. It's not just your future they show to everyone, they drag up painful moments from your past. Massive images and booming sound replay regrets, shameful experiences, humiliations. It's everywhere: pain, regret, anxiety. You feel claustrophobic as the assault intensifies. You feel sick. It's not just a sick feeling, it's serious sick, terminal sick.

Where are *you* in relation to your mind? Does your mind sometimes feel like it's sweltering in the heat and humidity of a street market in Nairobi? It's just too crowded, too much is happening. You're frantically trying to stay vigilant, to keep up but you feel threatened and vulnerable.

Perhaps your mind is a gentle, manicured garden and you diligently and expertly manage the weeds. You plant wisely knowing that each plant will take time to grow through the darkness of the soil, upwards into the light and outwards offering flowers or fruit. You have faith in what you've planted and you allay any doubts by consistently tending the beds, until after time, you enjoy the fragrance of the flowers, the delicious fruit and the dances of visiting birds and bees.

Is your mind like a wondrous intergalactic amalgamation of thoughts and energy? Does your mind appear to you like a multiverse that you might not fully understand but that you're beginning to navigate? Do any of these locations reflect your inner world? Did one of your inner critics refute any of the ideas arguing: "That's not *me; I'm Iceland - expansive and elusive*".

I'm using the inner critic as a collective noun for a range of voices. Each voice will take precedence at various times in the day. Don't let your inner critic sabotage your intention for change. I heard a client say, "My inner critic isn't a landscape it's a washing machine. Spinning, spinning, ruminating, ruminating. I spin around worrying about this, that and the next and I find at the end of all the worrying that I've got nothing done and I'm absolutely shattered".

Give your inner critic a moment to describe how it perceives itself. What comes up? Even judgement about how futile or foolish my suggestions seemingly have been can reveal the tone of the inner critic that is most notable for you at the moment.

Whatever our mental environment, we more often than not leave thoughts unchallenged because we don't know that we can actually challenge them. Have you ever considered that your thoughts are behaving uncontrollably and disruptively? If you no longer want thoughts to run amok one of the first strategies you could try would be to take a moment to tune into the thoughts themselves. It won't be too long before one of the inner critics is criticising this essay, for whatever reason. One might argue that it is a vacuous metaphor and that there are several other ways to depict the inner world. Another might be dismissive and reluctant. Just notice what they are saying, and how they are saying it.

My suggestion is that there are land, sea and cityscapes of the mind. Identify where you are. Sometimes it's a dry, arid place. Sometimes you feel like you're drowning. Mindfulness gives you the awareness to be in the moment and ascertain what kind of location you're in. It can shift. It can transition from disaster to delight. Play a little. Get more light-hearted about it. It's hard to hit a moving target, so slow down and get deliberate about projecting your dreams onto those big screens. Imagine the joy of what you'd like in your life. Create vibrant, crystal clear images and a happy soundtrack. Watch your dreams take shape and keep returning to the scene, enlivening your mental landscape, with the people, places, experiences and things that you would like in your life. Self-acceptance and kind, affirming inner dialogue create happy mental landscapes.

Mind Over Natter will explore these and many more concepts, techniques and mindful meditations!

ACKNOWLEDGMENTS

To my sister, Lisa
You are the kindest, most loving and creative person I know. Thank you for your patience and generosity. I appreciate everything about you—especially that raucous laughter and the joy of your art! Thank you for holding me up when I was stuck in the darkness.

To my father, Roy
When you'd recite poems or read stories, you animated them in such a way that I believed in them wholeheartedly. Thank you for passing on your love of words.

To my late mother, Anne
I'm sad that you never got to read this book, the Mom. I know you'd have told everyone to read it as you fluffed out your tail feathers.

To my Son, Jesse
Remember when you'd lie on my chest watching TV and ask, "Are you crying Mummty?" My emotions flow freely around you. I pray for your resilience, health, wealth, love and happiness.

To Rana Eschur
I treasure our friendship. I appreciate your talent and your candour, it's helped me build up my resilience. Thank you for your time, dedication and advice in getting this book to a new level.

To Family and Friends
We're a bit of an eclectic bunch, scattered around the world, aren't we? Thank you for your influence.

To Felicity Fox
Thank you for the first edit. I should send you a punctuation repair kit for all my grammar gremlins! Thank you for your reassurance and enthusiasm.

To Dr Madan Kataria
Thank you for teaching me the joy of Laughter Yoga. Learning from you has been an honour. I truly appreciate your Foreword and all the life advice you've shared.

To Kary Oberbrunner
It's been a lifelong dream to write and publish a book. Thank you for the opportunity.

To Tina Morlock
Thank you for your encouragement and all your suggestions. I appreciate your overview of this book.

To Nanette O'Neal
I really value your first impressions and for believing in this topic and the way I express myself. It was so affirming for me that you believed in it right at the start, thank you.

Acknowledgments

To Clients
Your journey matters to me. I've learnt as much from you as you have from me. I hope you continue to thrive.

To Launch Team
Carol Jackson, Colleen Bird, Dallace Rickson Jolly, Elzabé Boshoff, Joy Miskimmin, Julie Granville, Laura Artico, Lisa Kane, Michelle Horner, Pauline May, Rana Eschur, Rob Hall, Sally Perrow, and Susanne Montgomery. Thank you, for reading the rough bits, sharing your stories and giving your feedback, this has been an amazing journey, your input is invaluable.

To You, Fabulous Reader
I wave my pom-poms for you because I believe change is possible and I want to cheer you along! I hope this book gives you some memorable tips to help you overcome your negative inner critics and harness the power of your positive ones. Let's meet again in my next book or at a workshop, event, online course, or seminar—soon!

Go for it!

INTRODUCTION—WHAT DOES MIND OVER NATTER MEAN?

"The hardest prison to escape is in your own mind."

Ronit Baras

What Can You Expect from This Book?

You can expect tangible and personal transformational tips, fresh new meditations, original poems I wrote to open each chapter, valuable insights, and hopefully a smile or two. Plus, I hope you'll feel you've found a tribe and you belong.

Why Did I Write It?

The darn thing kept harassing me! Seriously. I first wrote a version of this book in 2006 called, *Rise and Be Abundantly You*. I commissioned artists to design a crest as the cover of the book, which was a doodle fest of colourful sketches, heartfelt handwritten notes, pull outs, and ideas like those old-fashioned journals the Victorians used on their travels. I marvelled at those books as a child. I loved the blend of diary, scientific annotation, creative expression, and general observation. I stuck my professionally designed cover on an A4 hardcover note book and covered it with that super sticky see-through plastic, trying my best not to trap air bubbles. I've always dreamed of being a writer. In my twenties, I wrote for television, developing characters who hadn't even been cast yet. I simply used my imagination and the formulaic writing of the three act/thirty-minute TV sitcom structure. It was so exciting writing for producers and directors who worked in film and TV, and I got to interact with them, bounce ideas off them, and took their suggestions to heart. It was a phase in my life where I was unhindered by fear or doubt, and I simply stayed open like a channel receiving and giving creative ideas. I penned a couple of feature film scripts (that never went to production), a book (I didn't even entertain being published), another book of presentation skills (paid a fortune for the design and artwork but never published it), song lyrics (one of which I did release on a commercial CD), and poetry that I'd write as laments. Poetry doesn't have to be sad or serious, but when I feel that way, sometimes writing poetry can be cathartic. I allowed fear and doubt to stall my creativity, even before it had fully formed. The irony was, I included fear and doubt in *Rise and Be Abundantly You*, but I was so busy talking the talk I wasn't walking the walk.

I couldn't resist the ideas that kept bombarding me for *Rise*. They'd wake me at three in the morning! Ideas rising out of consciousness into my waking mind. It was a personal transformation book full of sketches and colour. I was so devoted to that book; I even took it away on holiday. Then, as luck—or perhaps my mindlessness—would have it, I lost it. That was a period in my life where I lost things: keys, jewellery, time, myself. I wasn't fully present which manifested as absentmindedness. My inner critics weren't happy about losing *Rise and Be Abundantly You*, and one by one they piled on their judgements:

Absentmindedness? Try ineptness! Inattentiveness!
Carelessness!
Just plain stupid!
You've lost the only copy.
Why didn't you digitally save it?
Now what?
Wake up!
Feckin eejit!

The cover of that book featured a phoenix in the centre of a crest and the content inside rose up in me once again, insisting it wanted to ascend once more. I'd concede to a re-write here and there, but my self-doubt would get the better of me, and I'd leave it. I had to move out of the way a bit and become a conduit for the ideas that have been trying to get my attention. My writing angels are persistent. Despite some massive upheaval over the last couple of years, this time I heeded their call and wrote not just from my heart, but rather *with* my heart since the message wasn't coming from me, but through me.

If you're standing at a threshold in your life and you're not sure what to do, I really hope this book offers you clarity. If you haven't found anything to light you up, perhaps you've been looking in the wrong place. Try noticing the illumination within you.

Don't feel alone—we've all hotly pursued "fixes" that will make us richer, stronger, thinner, smarter, taller, shorter, younger, older, etc. When people said I was the solution to my own problems, I wanted to explode because I knew for a fact that I wasn't good enough, and they didn't know just how much of an imposter I really was! Also, I didn't find it helpful to hear I was the solution to my own problems since clearly, I hadn't been given the secret key. Otherwise, I'd have used it by now.

I was confused. I didn't know how to access the mysterious, *inner me* solution zone. If people have said the same to you and you've been equally unable to navigate to self-mastery, I get your frustration. This probably isn't the first time you've thought about making changes. I didn't know what to do or how to do it, only that something was wrong, and I had to do something about it. The good news is I'm not going to get all cryptic and expect you to join the dots. If I can help you, I'll hold nothing back. What will it take for you to give it a try? If you're already feeling the tug of resistance, that's a sign to read on. It'll be a mixed bag, but give it a go anyway. Embrace variety, expect contrast, discover, or uncover your resilience.

It doesn't take high intellect for any of us to look around and notice we're not where we thought we would be at this stage in our lives. The bestseller lists can sometimes be confusing since there are as many experts and gurus as there are problems. Who's the right fit for you? What strategies can you believe in, and how quickly can you implement them to change your life? You want support, but you don't want to feel judged. You want advice, but you don't want to feel forced. You want suggestions, but you want flexibility so you can adapt things to suit you. You want something that's possible, tangible, viable, not too hard, but enough of an assist to feel like you're making progress.

If your inner critics have already been nattering as you flick through these pages, perhaps that's a sign to give *Mind Over Natter* a whirl. If it's not the one for you, I won't be upset at all. In fact, I'll be delighted since you have clarity. Your clarity matters. Ask yourself, *why isn't it for me?* Wait until your mind

Introduction — What Does Mind Over Natter mean?

or your heart gives you the answer, then do that. If you're still here, that's fantastic; it's a sign that you're not alone.

We're all in this together.

If we're all in this together:

- We'd stop trying to get ahead by dominating, crushing, and destroying.
- We'd cease competing in favour of assisting.
- We'd ban blame and boost praise.

An image can instantaneously express layers of intertextual meaning. Not all pictures are created equal. Here's a picture of our Dalmatian, Keegan. She developed a massive liver tumour and sadly passed away at age nine. Dalmatians live up to fifteen years and sometimes beyond. I mourn her daily; she was a great girl. Why did I give my spotty girl a boy's name? In 2010, I was in a "K" craze. I had a Kawasaki super-bike named Keiko (yes, I name my vehicles). I cable tied my fluffy toy dragon named Kevin to my back seat as my permanent pillion so I never rode alone. Under the back-wheel guard, I fastened a small bell to remind me never to ride faster than my guardian angel could fly. I hadn't been in the market for a Dalmatian but the opportunity arose. Being of Irish descent, I wanted an Irish sounding name, so I chose Keegan.

Keegan

This is our other dog, Rhiley. He's six months older than Keegan (prior to the "K" phase).

Rhiley Blu

The Rhiley sketch, is by my artist sister, Lisa Kane, the official illustrator of *Mind Over Natter*. The natural instinct is to make a comparison between the images. It's easy to tell the difference between my simple line drawing and the more fully developed sketch by Lisa. If I sketched more often and honed the skill, I could probably develop a more rounded image. That's the great gift of life—it's constantly unfolding and perpetually improving. I encourage you to doodle for no reason whatsoever except that you can. Get a crayon, pen, or a pencil in your hand again. Draw something, anything, even a stick person. We spend a lot of time analysing and using a scientific mindset. But by colouring or drawing, you are shifting your mind into a creative hemisphere that will augment your creativity for life in general. People assume creativity is limited to artists, but we are all creative. You just have to find your creative outlet! After all, even navigating traffic takes creative energy.

Mindfulness doesn't refute the difference between the two sketches. What it suggests is a closer focus on the tone and quality of the observation. Being aware of comparison with non-judgmental curiosity is actually a refreshing way to live. Mindfulness encourages presence—just being with an idea, a feeling, an experience, a circumstance. Mindfulness invites noticing, not judging. It's impossible for us not to compare but it lightens our mental and emotional load when we pay attention to the tone of the comparison. If we look with our hearts, we can see differences rather than judging something as inferior or superior. Science is confirming that the mere act of observation changes the object being observed. It works the other way too. You've no doubt experienced a state change based on observations in memory, imagination, or what's in front of you. Can you feel your body react when I suggest taking a bite of a lemon right through the skin and into that sour flesh? I get a saliva surge in my mouth even just thinking about it.

Being mindful is a practice of presence, of noticing and extending awareness. Did you notice Keegan has two different coloured eyes? Even though they're black and white sketches, if you take a closer look, you might be able to see the difference more clearly now that you know. I can't tell you how many people mindlessly (albeit enthusiastically) said, "Oh, she has one eye." They meant she has one blue eye or one brown eye, but what they said was something else. To understand more about mindfulness, it's sometimes easier to go via the portal of mindlessness. We're more mindless than we realise.

Would it surprise you to learn that you were born mindful and became increasingly more mindless through education and conditioning? Professor Ellen J. Langer is a pioneer of scientific mindfulness research. She's intelligent, insightful, wise, creative, and amusing. As Dan Ariely, author of *Predictably Irrational,* writes, "Ellen Langer's research changed the face of psychology …She also made the cosmos smile." In the 2014 Preface to her 25th Anniversary Edition of *Mindfulness,* Langer says:

> In the 1970s, as social psychology was experiencing what was called "the cognitive revolution," studying the kinds of thoughts people were having, I began to wonder whether people were

thinking at all. Decades of research later, I have found the answer to be a resounding NO. Mindlessness is pervasive. In fact, I believe virtually all of our problems—personal, interpersonal, professional, and societal—either directly or indirectly stem from mindlessness.[1]

When you read any of Langer's material, you'll be struck by her clarity and her interest in enquiring a few layers deeper than the obvious questions about what motivates us and how we make decisions. You'll also be surprised at how relatively effortless it is to become receptive to intuition and mindfulness. She says, "Both are reached by escaping the heavy, single-minded striving of most ordinary life." She opened my mind to how differently we could engage in the process of creative thinking and how "the teaching of facts as absolute truth can lead to mindlessness". Much of what we automatically do in our lives is based on past patterns or things we were taught and haven't been able to adapt into new concepts.

Langer expands on this:

> When our minds are set on one thing or on one way of doing things, mindlessly determined in the past, we blot out intuition and miss much of the present world around us. If Archimedes had had his mind set only on taking a bath, he would probably not have discovered the displacement of water. By keeping free of mindsets, even for a moment, we may be open to see clearly and deeply.[2]

Toddler Wisdom

I love the way toddlers approach life because they haven't fully developed a mindset; they're so changeable. Do toddlers interrogate their intentions? No, they just do stuff. When they spill their food, or knock their juice over, does a toddler ask, "Why me?" We call it the "Terrible Two's" but toddlers don't label their emotions. Imagine a toddler learning to walk and after her first fall, quits concluding it's clearly unmanageable, blaming her parents, and drowning her sorrows in her bottle.

When they draw, do toddlers ever hesitate? Do they feel disappointed in themselves for imperfect squiggles? Do toddlers perpetuate the piffle in artist statements to justify their splodges? Do they get caught up in existential angst about the pathway not lining up with the front door? Hang on a minute. Is it a pathway, a stem, a river, a ribbon? Who knows? Who cares? They don't invest so much anxiety into their efforts. That's our adult domain. That's what we do to ourselves after years of conditioning and self-criticism.

When we're new in the world, our imagination is easily accessible. We don't limit ourselves; we dabble in all sorts of tasks because we have a beginner's mind—stuff is interesting, and we're keen to keep learning. These are the qualities we lack as adults. We lose our sense of creativity, resilience, and wonder. Later in life, some of us become exponents of an inflated self-awareness, exaggerating our appearance, acquisitions, and achievements. We see others doing it and feel it's impossible for us to keep up.

Without possibility, we lose hope. Whether we feel hopeful or hopeless, it starts in our minds. I felt hopeless because I had a destructive self-image for the majority of my life. Our self-image isn't limited to our appearance. It pertains to our identity in general, what we like, who we're like, and vice versa. As it turns out, I did find that the solutions to my problems were inside me, but I didn't know that when I started. If I can shorten the discovery time for you, wouldn't that be worthwhile since we're in this together? Our journey is of perennial learning, living, loving, healing, and sharing. I want to participate by offering ideas that helped me heal. My objective isn't to cut short your lessons, impede your growth, or deny your lived experience. It's to shine a light for you so you can consciously choose where to go next. If we're all about the destination, there'll be a vast number of roses left un-smelled. I was at a rose show recently, and those perfumes are as satisfying as they're subtle. Being with the roses was enough. I didn't long for lilies or wish for wisteria because I was fully present with the roses. That's another insight of mindfulness, the beauty of *enough*.

What Does Mind Over Natter Mean?

People who hear voices in their head are deemed insane. If that's the case, then aren't we all a little crazy? We hear loads of voices all the time—things we hear from our parents, teachers, family, friends, books, song lyrics, TV shows, advertising, social media, films, jokes, quotes, speeches, memories. Our voice is nattering along all day in a never-ending running commentary of what's happening. What should be happening, what might have happened, what should never have happened, and what terrifying thing might still happen.

To natter is to talk casually, especially about trivial matters. To chatter seems more light-hearted than to natter. Maybe it's the alliteration, but nattering seems to evoke a sense of nagging. It's the persistent nagging of the inner voice that I've depicted in the book title. The phrase "Mind over matter," infers the power of the mind to overcome difficult thoughts and situations. If you have a stitch during athletics training, your coach might shout across the track, "It's mind over matter—keep going!" Ever have to endure foul-tasting medicine as a child? A parent may have suggested, "It's mind over matter—get that down, you." The premise of *Mind Over Natter* is an enquiry into our mind, how it functions, what it allows into awareness, and then to gain control of the mind by usurping the negative nattering.

My invitation is to observe the mind with curiosity, not condemnation. I like to use humour and stories to interpret what's going on upstairs. We can use that knowledge to access awareness to overcome the noise of the internal dialogue produced inside the mind. Fears, regrets, judgments etc., tumble around in a mental-washing machine that doesn't produce clean thoughts, only more filthy ones that hurt. Seldom is it a happy, encouraging, internal voice. The relieving truth is we can clean up our thinking when there *is* a positive voice in there—it's significant and

Introduction—What Does Mind Over Natter mean?

increasingly more available to us. I love this voice. I've noticed it speaks to me in the second person. On the way to the toilet, *"You've got your phone in your back pocket," is* a timely warning since I've destroyed more than my fair share of phones by mindlessly tipping them out of my back pocket into the loo. Have I done it more than once? Yes, I'm a slow learner. Correction—that's not true, I used to be, but now I'm an interested learner.

I've lost phones from boats, bikes, and even my swimming pool. The negative inner critic doesn't laugh at mistakes, it gets irate. The kinder inner critic, makes suggestions, offers hints, reminders, etc. You might hear these as intuition. I'll help you turn the volume up so you can hear intuitive messages more clearly.

My second intention is to usher that expansive, optimistic, encouraging, loving voice into a place of prominence and give you tips to access it so you can overcome difficult thoughts and situations. It's exhausting trying to overthrow the negative impact of a cruel internal dialogue. If you feel like your stress is getting out of control and you are ready to make some changes, you are closer than you think to getting your life together. Simply being aware that you're unhappy is a massive step. Most of us notice we're unhappy and stop there. Some people never make the distinction between their unhappiness and their ability to change it. Our thoughts are creating our lives. You can continue to blame others, call yourself a victim of circumstance, location, upbringing—or you can change your mind. Awareness is the first step towards transformation. Compassion for yourself (including your past and your future) is the next step. *Mind Over Natter* will help you harness the power of your mind to work *with* you and *for* you, not against you.

For many of us, internal voices chastise and criticize, and we don't fight them. We believe we're trapped in the awful self-fulfilling cycle they perpetuate. If you had to eat your words, would they be delicious, or disgusting? Imagine the tasty treat of creating an internal dialogue that nourishes you from the inside out. Our task is to identify, reject, and replace the beliefs that no longer serve us with beliefs that create happier outcomes.

Mindfulness and Meditation

Meditation is a mental activity. It's a way of producing an internal environment that accesses a peaceful heart. Happiness, contrary to what we imagine, isn't derived from external sources but is a result of a peaceful mind. Mindfulness is the practice of observing the mind, a focused effort, the holding of one thing in awareness, continuously. Meditation is the practice we use to access mindfulness and to expand awareness from moment to moment. The more we train in meditation, the greater our opportunity to experience mindfulness and the spaciousness of an expansive, open mind, and heart. Meditation is deliberately drawing awareness into the body, away from conceptual thought, and into loving kindness. In meditation, we attempt to shepherd ourselves back to an experiential awakening of possibilities rather than ruminating in a stuck mind, repeating negative behaviour.

CHAPTER ONE
SOMETHING'S WRONG. AM I STUCK HERE FOREVER?

"If you wanna fly, you got to give up the shit that weighs you down."

Toni Morrison

Something's Wrong

Perception / R E A L I T Y—who decides?
I am the convergence and the d i v e r g e n c e
A fix of satisfaction or location eludes me.
I'm unhinging.
How can it be reduced, defined, contained?
Indiscernible, indistinct; the sleeping dreaming waking
Nightmare.
Am I the darkness? Am I stuck forever?
Suffocation, choking, doubt, fear,
Neglect, abandonment, isolation, derision, shame, sorrow, mourning, incapacity, loss,

                                        lost.

Pain sears my body, my heart, my psyche.
The hurting, the hurting.
I can neither escape nor decipher myself.
Whom do I ask?
Who knows?
Who answers?

Poetry vs Emojis

Are you an *I hate poetry* person? Many people are. Poetry slows us down long enough to realise we've been in a trance of non-awareness. The words that normally sit neatly in sentences jut out in poetry. They ask us to consciously think and feel more than usual. We don't want to think and feel more. In fact, we're trying to think and feel less. At no time in history has society ever been so riddled with ways to numb out our experience of life. We've never had so much global wealth and yet been so spiritually bereft, stuck in overwhelm, fear, and pain. Imbalance surrounds us—starvation, and scarcity persist, yet gluttony and waste pervade. Many of us become addicted, trapped, insatiable. We tell ourselves we don't have time, but we demand instant results.

> *Snap to it—give me five keys to happiness.*
> *Three steps to stress-free living.*
> *I'm multitasking. Catch my attention right this second or I'm gone!*

Words evoke thoughts, emotions, and feelings. They get pretty close but never quite capture our whole meaning. Words are an approximation, but at least they help us communicate. We're getting so lazy that we don't even bother speaking. We send pictures and videos and think they suffice. Ever misinterpreted an emoji and sent hands clapping when you meant *praying* after someone had died? We can't expect emojis to articulate what we're trying to say out loud. Poetry is another way of jolting us out of the trance of non-aware, auto-pilot living. The poems I've written for this book attempt to capture the tone of a mindset prior to the discovery of awareness. Their tone changes as my own transformation expands.

This is a book about transformation, but it doesn't take itself too seriously. None of us should. Elizabeth Gilbert says, "I've never seen a transformation that didn't begin with the person in question finally getting over their own bullshit." Yes, I believe it's time but don't get bogged down by the process or the information. I want you to enjoy yourself, have a giggle, take a look at who you are, and what you'd like to do differently. As soon as you slow down and step out of the noise of panic and chaos that defines most of our lives, your inner critics will probably show up and start attacking you. Be prepared is all I'm saying. I'll show you what to expect and how to handle the criticism.

Many people want top strategies for getting ahead. They search externally to appease what's happening inside. What's wrong in your life? Do you know? Is it a few things that cumulatively make you feel worse? Are you in debt? Have you lost your job? Do you feel desperately unhappy, overweight, unfit, stressed, tired, anxious, depressed, or angry? That was me before my first coffee of the day. It's probably true for most of us until we decide to make changes. I was also impatient, intolerant, self-pitying, self-loathing, unforgiving, and bitter. I was in bad shape in all respects of my life. It wasn't that *something* was wrong—*everything* was wrong. I came to see that everything was nothing if I didn't breathe life into it. Accusingly, I thought I was what was wrong. Enquiry showed me that I wasn't wrong as such, just my thinking was off. Wrong implies judgement—right or wrong. Mindfulness encourages non-judgmental awareness. Once I stopped rebuking myself and offered self-forgiveness and compassion, I began to see the patterns of thought that were creating my reality. Mindfulness gave me the tools to overcome the negative inner chatter in my mind. If I could get out of those doldrums, I'm convinced you can too.

It's time.
Allow yourself.
Let's get your dream life started.

Metrics Matter

Some of us struggle, but I genuinely do know my right from my left. I don't have to glance down and see which wrist is wearing the watch. I'm clear on North, South, East, and West, but when I'm using navigation on my phone, and it tells me to head east on Main Street when I haven't a cooking clue where I am to start from, I can lose it!

"Which way is East?"

It's important to know where you *are* in order to decide where you'd like to go. If you don't measure your progress, not only do you miss out on the joy of the journey, you also miss the chance to take corrective action. Sometimes how far you've come can fuel how far you've yet to go. When I'm stuck in a queue, glancing back at the people behind me gives me a sense of relief. I don't mean this in a smug way but as a means of reminding myself I was there, and I've come this much further already, and I'm making progress.

Starting is imperative, but measuring helps us to stay on track. Staying is where all the twists and turns happen. Staying is Act II of the three-act play. If you're not tracking where you are, you can't know if you're out of alignment. The contrast sets up the next expansion on the journey, so it's not a question of target, arrival, and end. It's more like a meandering spaghetti map of exploration. It's become a cliché to talk about destinations and journeys, but we truly put so much pressure on end goals that we deprive ourselves of lessons and insights along the way. It's not possible to start if you're still locked in a vague sense of unhappiness. Get clear on what's not working for you now and from that, you can get clear on what else you'd prefer. Then, start and stay and re-set along the way.

What's Really Going On?

When you take time to investigate what's really going on with you, that's where the magic happens. Instead of avoiding, delaying, or denying what's wrong, try accurately describing it. If you sense something is wrong in your life but you just can't put a finger on it, see if you can identify with any of the feelings expressed in that poem. If you skipped it, now might be a good time for you to acknowledge that you make a habit of skipping over stuff, and making assumptions. Getting to know who you are and what motivates you isn't an invitation for your inner critic to attack you. This is a book that wants to help you, and it may just achieve that if you are ready to take a deep, real, sincere, heartfelt look at where you are and what you've done to get there. Where you are isn't who you are, but it is a result of how you've been thinking and feeling. Transformation isn't just about making the change, it's about clarity on *why* there's a need for change.

How far into the poem did you notice your judgments and not the poem itself? Were you able to read the whole poem, or did your mind jump away to plans, memories, or any other distractions midway through? The reason I'm asking these questions is that I'm showing you how, in reading the poem, your inner voice was already chiming in. We all have an inner voice. Our inner voice "talks" to us. It doesn't need emojis to send us pictures of flames and bombs going off in our mind. It sets them off in thoughts and feelings that manifest in our lives.

The inner voice is commenting, noticing, distracting, judging, reminding, warning, arguing, remembering, and ruminating. It's nattering consistently and perpetually, minute by minute, hour after hour, day after day. It only stops when we sleep. During rest, the subconscious mind takes over and gives the conscious mind time to rest. Whilst the conscious mind is functioning, it is also deleting certain experiences it doesn't regard as pertinent because it wouldn't have time to do what the unconscious mind does in controlling our physiology. Messages from our bodies are communicated through layers of consciousness to the inner voice that pipes up in the middle of a TV show, sex, or a business meeting. The messages say: *I'm starving! What's to eat? I think I'll paint the ceiling beige…*

Fear Is Our Mind's Way of Protecting Us

Our first encounter with anything new is an opportunity for our mind to race ahead to scan and detect threats. Then, our mind reacts—either in the form of a panic attack or a subtle lane change. It decides: proceed, escape or collapse. The mind is keen to warn us, eliminate the hazard, and keep us safe. The mind uses fear as a protective mechanism. Fear evokes impactful, immediate action to fight or flee or freeze. Our mind is highly protective. It shoots down anything it doesn't know or trust, but the trouble with that philosophy is that it limits our growth. There's too much collateral damage. How can we expand if something new is obliterated before it has a chance to get through our mental protective barriers? How will anything be able to seep into our general non-judgmental and curious awareness? We don't know what we don't know!

You're Basically Alright

Time truly does build perspective. We think we're doomed but as Dr Rick Hanson says, we're basically alright. I'm vastly different from the person who set out to write this book. I've lost weight, purged physically, emotionally, mentally, and financially. I've let go some intimate relationships, learned to sleep better without pharmaceutical assistance, and found a joy for the life I'd contemplated ending. I've lost three significant loves: my precious mother, who died in our arms as my sister and I held her through her harrowing last hours, my beloved Dalmatian, Keegan, who was more a family member than pet, and our Weimaraner, Rhiley, so gentle and loving, who nurtured us through those deaths. My cousin died, and my best friend's daughter died in a series of unexpected awful events. Sometimes being surrounded by death helps us appreciate and value life.

The *Something's Wrong* poem reminds me how disjointed my head and my heart were. If you're struggling with pain and loss and in a difficult relationship with yourself, your intimate partner (or lack of said partner) your health, your family, your work, your finances, your spirituality, or whatever you're going through, you're basically alright, right here and right now. I would've rejected that premise in the past—nobody knew how bad it was for me; they didn't know my story. That's often our problem—we're so used to desperately holding on to our "story" we don't bother creating a new one.

If you want to ramp it up and enjoy a life of abundance that's beyond being basically alright, that's fantastic. I applaud that wholeheartedly, and I hope to show you how to do that. Nobody said you have to suffer, scrimp, and save. It's time to awaken into a joyful, playful, generous life! Our inner critics keep us oppressed then criticise us for being depressed.

Would you like to be?

Happier
Calmer
Kinder
Healthier
Wealthier
More patient
More resilient
More confident
More peaceful

And how about being able to sleep easier and more deeply in a refreshing, rejuvenating rest that sets you up for another superstar day in your life?

Wouldn't It Be Cool vs What If

Ever noticed how rinsing sand from a bath takes a few go's? You have to keep rinsing and rinsing. That's what transformation is like—continually rinsing away negative self-limiting beliefs and allowing new questions to wash over you. Wouldn't it be cool to find yourself asking different questions? I love the "wouldn't it be cool?" game since it allows us to get playful in our minds. We're so used to piling up the "what ifs?" when we imagine doomsday scenarios of everything that might go wrong. *What if?* and *wouldn't it be cool?* both exist in the imagination. One makes you feel rotten in the present and seems to threaten a worse future, while the other makes you feel better in the present and ushers in a better future. Which one would you prefer to play? Your mind is playing this game with or without your consent, so take ownership and direct your life rather than being a victim to negative thinking and all the awfulness it attracts.

What if... vs Wouldn't it be cool!

What if...	Wouldn't it be cool...
...it's too late?	...to know this is the perfect time right now?
...I can't get out of this negative mindset?	...that, no matter what, I keep bouncing back?
...I just can't do it?	...if amazing ideas just came to me?
...nobody will ever love me?	...to be so loving to myself that the right people are attracted to me?
...I'm really not good enough?	...to be the embodiment of everything I admire?
...I'm just never going to make it?	...to excel at everything I do, even beyond anything I've ever imagined?

"Wouldn't it be cool?" is a lovely way to start using your inner voice to search for positive responses to questions that normally leave you feeling sick about yourself. This game is easier to play than you think, and it opens up the first exercise to encourage your mind to overcome your negative inner chatter.

Background on Exercises: Do Them, They Will Supercharge Your Transformation

Journaling and meditation are essential features of *Mind Over Natter*. Read the meditations out loud or in your mind. You might even like to record them for yourself if it would benefit you to hear them in your own voice. The scripts are available at the end of each chapter. I've voiced them for you so you can relax and listen to the audio. Links on https://www.tovekane.com for you to enjoy as guided audio and video versions of the meditations. That's coming up later. For now, a quick note about journaling.

Get yourself a beautiful journal. Cover it with something that inspires and delights you. Don't go drab—that doesn't excite your creative mind. This is the start of your transformation—don't start with limits! There's a magical moment when you put a pen in your hand and touch it down on paper. It's tactile, it's full of potential, and it has the power to surprise and move you. Think it and ink it. For your own sake, *do* the exercises. Thinking isn't doing. It's not enough to glance over them and think you've got it. I warmly encourage you to do the exercises as we go along; your insights will be invaluable.

Can't I just type? your inner voice might ask. The answer is: better to hand write. I love whirring over my keyboard as much as the next person, but when you go old school, it slows you down, slows down your mind, puts you into your body, and allows you to get creative. As you form the letters by hand, you enhance your awareness. Take your time—rushing is part of our problem— it's a reason we get stressed. Also, who's to say you don't draw a doodle or sketch an image that intrigues you or expresses your feelings? You will benefit from engaging in the practices and meditations. They'll supercharge your experience of this book and help you gain power over mind natter.

Exercise: What If vs Wouldn't It Be Cool?

In a spirit of creative playfulness, List or draw your Top 10 **"what ifs."**

Clue: They're usually laden with anxiety or dread.

Then, have a great time rephrasing them as, **"wouldn't it be cool?**

Clue: They don't have to be realistic, but if they are, isn't that cool, too?

For example:

What if...

1. What if... nobody buys *Mind Over Natter*?
2. What if... my son is in danger at work?
3. What if... I get sick again?
4. What if... I fall in love but work separates us?
5. What if... my investments collapse in a market crash?

Wouldn't it be cool if...

1. Wouldn't it be cool if... even one person bought *Mind Over Natter* and it helped her transform her life?
2. Wouldn't it be cool if... my son felt safe at work, and he could take swift action to protect himself and others?

3. Wouldn't it be cool if… I looked after my WHOLE self – mind, body, and spirit?

4. Wouldn't it be cool… to enjoy love that knows no boundaries?

5. Wouldn't it be cool… to be so abundant, that no matter what, I will always have enough?

Why the Voices Matter

What we think and say and feel is what we experience in life. There's a direct correlation between the content of our inner voice and how we relate to the voice and the conditions in our outer world. The impact of the inner voice is irrefutable. Here is a significant distinction: the inner critic is an aspect of the inner voice; it doesn't occupy the whole domain of our conscious awareness. We'll explore this expanded sense of awareness later and that will lead to a contemplation on the mind not being fixed in the brain.

The inner voice is constantly observing and commentating. The negative inner critic is that part of the voice that's aligned with a negative bias. There's also an optimistic voice—a personal cheerleader, coach, a BFF—a benevolent voice of love and kindness. The negative inner critic has hogged the limelight for so long that it seems more dominant, and therefore, its impact appears more prevalent but that's the trick it plays on us. Through enquiry, you'll come to see that there's more to life than the negative critic's jibes. Imagine how amazing your life could be if you were constantly being encouraged and guided in a positive way that made you feel excited and hopeful? Some inner critics make us feel discomfort at such a thought, like optimism is implausible.

Picture a Light-Filled Room.

Imagine you are inside a wooden cabin, built from tall trees, and you can still smell the scent of freshly cut pine. The ceiling, walls, and floor are fitted and joined flawlessly. The cabin is aglow with gold-amber sunlight that streams through streak-free windows. Beams of light illuminate dust particles dancing on a breath of air. It's an inanimate space, yet warmth and hope somehow reside in the radiance. The trees that lived once, seem reborn as they shape the room, protecting.

Imagine a dark space in the cabin. Your mind might resist darkness if the light appealed to you. (I think I may have been in a small trance, fully responsive to the light in the cabin. Although since we've interrupted programming for this quick chat, I also wondered how many trees had been cut to make the cabin and had they come from a sustainable source? See what I mean? The mind doesn't stop. The inner dialogue is running all the time, even when we're focused on building a scene in our imagination. Back to the cabin…) Mine is on the edge of a mountain, and I can vaguely see the azure blue of a glacier, its snow melting in trickles that will river to the sea.

To contemplate a single, dark space in a room filled with light doesn't significantly detract from the light in the room. The power of radiance dominates. Did your mind create the dark space as a dark corner in the cabin? Was your dark space an entrance to a basement? Was the dark space a contained structure like a dark stove? Or was it a levitating black quadrant in the middle of the luminosity surrounding it?

Imagine Darkness

Swap the image. Imagine darkness. Is it encroaching? In the dark, fear rises. Is it a recess in your mind—deep, dark, intangible? Perhaps rather than delving too deeply into your mind, visualise a dark room—let's say a basement—where no natural light is possible. Zero light is darker than you think.

Now - light a small candle. It doesn't matter if it's in the corner or the centre, the whole room takes on the flickering illumination of that candle. I can't see this image without glorious Barbra Streisand singing "Papa can you hear me?" and now, neither can you. You're welcome. The point is—it's much harder to darken light and much easier to lighten dark. Our inner critic is a dark aspect of our inner voice. Since we haven't lit a candle of encouragement, hope, kindness, compassion, (insert any positive emotion), we haven't experienced the swift illumination of how much lighter things can be. When we offer anything that's slightly higher on the scale of emotions, slightly lighter out of dark thoughts, we have a greater chance of filling the room of our mind with the light of understanding.

Transform from Dark to Light

If you've given credence to your inner critic, it might be a relief to know that you can offer the same belief and acceptance to the inner, positive voice, too. Through awareness and gradual practice, anyone can transform the negative viewpoint of the inner critic into a positive, creative energy that can work for good. We've become habitual thinkers, and our life has followed the pattern of that same-old-same-old thinking. So how do we change the habitual thoughts? Habits are hard to break, aren't they? Not really, they're just patterns, and new ones can replace ineffective ones, if you're willing. Through neuro-plasticity we can actively change our minds, change our thoughts, and by extension, the cumulative effect of those thoughts i.e. how they show up in our lives and how we experience the world. It's not enough to recognise that we want to change, we need to take action. Let me rephrase that, instead of: "we need" or "we should" or "we must" take action, start by saying, "we **get** to take action." That makes it seem more fun, more like a game, something you feel like doing and not merely a dictate to be obeyed.

Change is a process, and momentum is key. We can't jump from a speeding negative thought train and expect to land safely on a speeding positive thought train heading the opposite way. Our fast-paced world is one of instant gratification, and this fosters unreasonable expectations. We demand that change be immediate. Part of our pain and suffering lies in the fact that change, for a variety of excellent reasons, takes time. In order to fire up new thoughts and neural pathways, it's important to know our existing patterns. Isn't it exciting to see how science itself has changed? We were told we have a finite brain capacity and that we sequentially lose that capacity after attaining our maximum learning phase in our late teens. Now we know—neural pathways are firing up throughout our lifetime, which means we *can* teach an old dog new tricks. If what you've created in your life no longer serves you, stop chewing on that old bone. It's time to change. By identifying our go-to behaviour, we can learn what our new preference could be.

Negative Limiting Beliefs

Many of us are clueless about triggers or what drives our behaviours. This is why self-acceptance and self-compassion are such precious allies in the war against our negative inner critics. I know we're supposed to talk peace, and Mother Theresa famously used to decline anti-war rallies in favour of attending peaceful gatherings. It's not merely semantics. It refers to a mindset and an energy orientation. How we phrase things matters. What we resist persists. I use the analogy of a fight because it is more easily accessible at this early stage in transformation. Make no mistake, there's an undeniable conflict and you're being compelled by your future self to prevail.

Be kinder to yourself! Getting caught up in berating yourself for previous negative thoughts is hardly a positive way of redirecting those thoughts. Life has caused us to accumulate numerous beliefs. I say accumulate rather than form, since most of the beliefs we consider to be our own have merely been observed and assimilated. We think of them as our beliefs but they're no more ours than our breath. The breath is a life-force available to every living creature on land, sea, and air. We benefit from the breath but we don't own the breath or keep the breath since it is in constant flux.

We didn't create the air we breathe; it's gifted to us. However, we're responsible for polluting the air on the planet, just like our thoughts and beliefs are polluted. It's time to detox negative thoughts and beliefs. There's a high probability that you didn't create your beliefs. It's more likely they've been passed on to you. You may not have agreed with some of your parents' beliefs and those clashes were the fodder of heartache as you grew into yourself and away from their mindset. Your beliefs about yourself were instilled in you by influential figures in your childhood: parents/caregivers, family, teachers, religious environments, friends, society, and the media. You may not have shared their opinion or you may have been caught, hook, line, and sinker, flapping and gasping till you acquiesced before they tossed you back into life. Even your beliefs about God are likely to have been passed on to you. Beliefs form the keystone of our values and behaviours, and yet many of us have never consciously interrogated the validity or applicability of our beliefs. They've become so ingrained that we take our beliefs to be the actual truth. We believe our beliefs. It's one thing to have a belief that you have consciously accepted in your life, but many of us have several unconscious or subconscious beliefs floating around in our psyche. We assume that these beliefs are our reality. They impact our reality, and they impede change! We have to first identify the beliefs that are not working for us anymore and then change or delete them from our experience.

Can you recognise some of these negative, limiting beliefs?

I'm not good enough.
Nobody loves me.
I don't have enough time.
I don't have enough money.
I can't do that.

People-Pleasing

Many of us share the belief that if we do enough people-pleasing, then people will accept us. Our need for perpetual nourishment applies to body, mind, and soul.

• • •

I'm nine years old, already an old hand at people-pleasing. I can swim the length of a twenty-five-meter-long school swimming pool, underwater. There's this teacher I idolise. She's a goddess. I don't blame myself—everyone adores her. She's equally popular in the classroom and as an extra mural coach—swimming, athletics, and hockey. I'd do anything for her.

We're doing swim drills, and it's close to the end of the session. It's a late summer's afternoon, the sun is lighting and darkening behind clouds. It's not going to rain. Sometimes, when it does rain, we huddle in the corner of the pool where the water is warmer than the air outside. I can smell fresh cut grass. The sound of a lawn mower is drowned out by the noise of kicking and splashing and swimmers egging each other on. I see Miss H and another teacher approach. I know how Miss H is feeling depending on her walk. Sometimes she strides out and I know she's happy. Today she's walking slowly, planning for the next interschools swim event. Our school swimming pool is made of floor-to-wall lilac tiles, which become blue under the African sky. "Look what she can do." Miss H elbows her colleague. I've been kicking my heart out behind a board, which I chuck to the side of the pool. When asked to perform, I push my people-pleasing pedal to the metal. Without stopping to compose myself, I snatch a quick, deep breath, duck under the water, and whoosh! An almighty kick off the tiles in my underwater people-pleasing pursuit.

I mentioned the pool was made of tiles. They're not famous for traction. My foot slips as I kick for that big launch. Plus, I hadn't closed my mouth properly, so half of that breath is water. I scrape my toes so painfully against the tiles, I'm wincing underwater. Pain literally takes my breath away and I lose valuable air as bubbles escape. Underwater breaststroke, gliding just centimetres off the bottom of the pool. Sometimes my knee bashes the bottom. I don't have goggles, but I don't need to see where I'm going. I'm not looking because I'm engrossed in my headspace. I'm pulling for the far wall. I'm fatigued after the drills. My lungs are bursting, and my eyes are blurring. I know my lungs can't take much more. Each stroke pressures my chest. I can't fail.

My little body is at its limit. *She's going to be so proud of me.* I'm devoted to Miss H. I crave her attention. I want her to see me and love me. *Pull, glide, kick. Pull, glide, kick.* I start saying these words in my mind. Then, I can hear a sound coming from my throat, and it's not the words. It's like a bursting, desperate underwater begging. Midway, my heart is pounding, and my brain is begging me to stop. But my mind is pressing on. There's an argument in my head, *Surface! No don't! Pull, glide, kick. This is nuts. You're going to pass out. Push! Keep going! If you want her to like you, you'd better keep going! Pull, glide, kick. You can't do it. You should have taken a proper breath. You're such a loser. Pull, glide, kick. You're not going to make it. Just give up and stop being so pathetic.*

I can see their blurry figures walking along the side of the pool. They've seen my strokes but not my struggle. The wall—I can see the wall! I reach for it on the edge of fainting. My legs are too heavy to kick up. I surface somehow and as my head cuts through the water canopy, I heave, heavily for air but pretend not to. They say in unison, "Wow, well done," and then carry on with their discussion.

• • •

People aren't nearly as invested in us as we might assume. The voice in my head driving me on was not the voice of the coaches. They were curious, but not expectant, and certainly not as cruel and demanding as that voice had been. I stood up and caught my breath. The other swimmers merely swam around me as the drills continued. I was utterly spent. As little as I was, I felt smaller as my effort seemed insignificant. Worse, it was irrelevant. That was when some of the first nattering loops took hold in my mind. A range of voices all hissing and cursing at me:

You don't matter.
You don't make any difference.
You think anybody cares about you?
What were you thinking?
You nearly drowned you feckin eejit!

If you've ever felt that way, like you were less than—it's okay—take a deep breath. Those are the voices of the negative inner critics. Listen carefully, the positive ones are in there, too:

Wow!
You did it.
That was hard.
Look at what you can do.
You've got skills, kid.

People-pleasing ensures our survival. Not too long ago, getting into trouble with the tribe meant expulsion. Being excluded from the safety of numbers meant rejection, isolation, abandonment, and vulnerability not only as emotional experiences but with potentially deadly outcomes. If you've been a people-pleaser and you think it's fashionable to berate yourself about it because others say so, might I suggest you were doing what came naturally? Be a little less harsh on yourself. Don't push so hard. There's no need to risk drowning to please others, and don't drown yourself in criticism. Confidence and self-worth are just a few of the incredible benefits to gain in getting your mind over the nattering. Through the use of present moment awareness in mindfulness, you'll build resilience, patience, and a sense of compassion for yourself and everyone around you.

Mindfulness

Focus Less on People—Pleasing and Protect What Pleases You

This book is about identifying those cruel mental loops that grind us out of happiness and cause massive stress in our lives. We can replace them with kinder mental loops. Then, through mindfulness, we can find ways to restore our wellbeing to create calm, peace, joy, fun, and happiness. To what extent do we people-please and to what degree are we consciously aware that we do it? Have you ever met a person who's genuinely pleased by other people? No, most people bitch about others. You'd think we'd prefer to surround ourselves with people who preferred sharing ideas rather than bad news stories about everyone else.

*Lasting approval doesn't come
from the tribe.
It's how you feel
about yourself,
and it's fuelled by
self-compassion and intention.*

#mindovernatterbook

Most people-pleasing isn't actually solicited by others. They're generally too caught up in their negative mental talk to notice anyone else. How often have you assumed someone looked at you funny? Later, you discovered they'd been thinking about something at the office and whilst they looked at you, they hadn't really *seen* you? We sometimes jump to conclusions which allude more to our perception than the reality of the other person. We read into things based on how we're feeling. We offer people-pleasing as a means of securing acceptance, but we often do so from a vibration of self-loathing. So, we're not really convincing advocates, are we? If we got out of other people's business and got into our own experience and explored what makes us happy, we would be more attractive to people, which would negate our need to manage them. Provided you aren't harming yourself, others, or the environment, do what pleases you, and if it has the same effect on others, fantastic!

Mindfulness encourages us to be aware of our tendencies. Our thoughts produce associated beliefs, values, and feelings which impact our behaviour and the actions we take. If mindfulness isn't already a part of your life, you might be operating on autopilot. Rehashing default behaviour becomes an experience of life. But it isn't life as it can be. Patterns quickly become entrenched. The more we think a certain thought, the easier it becomes to dwell on it. The more we dwell on it, the thought manifests into a belief which shifts into feelings, behaviours, and ultimately into the world of form, and it becomes a reality. The fascinating thing about this principle of manifestation—thoughts become things—is that it's always working. We underestimate the significance of our choice—wanted or unwanted. Our decision often depends on our vibrational alignment. We attract what we think about most of the time. We can't stop thinking. When we aren't actively aware of our thoughts, they slide into negativity. The principle of manifestation is thoughts become things whether they're good thoughts to good things or bad thoughts to bad things. Mindfulness is the means of directing thinking towards preferred outcomes.

Good Vibrations

Science has repeatedly described that everything is vibrating in an energy-based universe. The difference between a table with a book on it or the hand lifting the book is simply a matter of atoms, the rate of vibration, and the space between them. We're really effective at manifesting stress and anxiety in our lives. Then, we complain about the repercussions of those feelings and how they create chaos and suffering. Have you ever wondered why we don't use the same enthusiasm to attract the things we'd prefer rather than the things we dread? Attraction and aversion involve the same principles. They expand and contract based on awareness and the amount of emotional energy we infuse into them. Have you ever noticed those people who refuse to cheer up after they moan to you about all their problems? They can be exasperating.

There's more that unites us than divides us. When I was in a deep depression, I assumed I was all alone, and no one else could relate to my experience. Mindfulness reminded me that other people can also feel this way. We all have encouraging or discouraging inner voices. Sometimes they praise us. Sometimes, they punish and persecute us. Mindfulness makes us aware of the voices and allows us to accept they exist. Accepting the voice isn't the same as condoning what it has to say. It is merely acknowledging its existence. Awareness can help calm stress responses, but when we're caught in the midst of chaos and upheaval, awareness is the furthest thing from our mind. We only know we feel acute anxiety. Becoming aware of anxious thinking is the starting point to slowing the momentum of those thoughts. Sometimes, a speeding train is all we have available. We've no idea how to slow or stop it and certainly no inkling about getting on a different train. Regaining mind over natter is slowing down long enough to give awareness a chance.

Awareness

Our first task is to have a sufficient level of awareness. What are we saying to ourselves? How are we saying it? When are we saying it? If you have a fierce inner critic who condemns you and doesn't comfort you, something's wrong. Why would anybody allow a cruel taskmaster to berate, demean, and condemn them? I don't believe negative motivation is good for anything, yet some people thrive on it. Whatever style appeals to you, to get from here to there, remember that life isn't linear, and I don't know when we developed the expectation it was. The sooner we embrace the twists and turns, the mischievous gremlins, and the ubiquitous Murphy's Law, which states, "Whatever can go wrong, will go wrong," we will be better prepared to continue the journey. The contrasts help us identify what we want based on what we don't want. The answer to the question, "Am I stuck here forever?" is, no—you might feel stuck but nothing is forever. Let's see how to get you unstuck. If you're anything like me, you're probably full of doubt. Do you want to doubt and stay stuck, or believe and dance in freedom?

Be Bright, Be Brief, Be Mindful

- This book is about identifying those cruel mental loops that grind us out of happiness and cause massive stress in our lives. It's also about replacing them with kinder mental loops.
- We can't expect emojis to express what we mean.
- Don't take yourself, or life, too seriously.
- We search *out there* to appease what's happening *in here*.
- Instead of avoiding, delaying, or denying what's wrong, honestly become aware of what's wrong.
- What if? vs Wouldn't it be cool? List your frightening thoughts and then list imaginative, positive, alternative outcomes that counteract those fears.
- Background on Practices—*do* them, they'll supercharge your transformation.
- Our thoughts, words, and feelings determine how we live our lives.
- Light-filled room vs imagining darkness.
- Replace we *need* or we *should* or we *must* take action with, we *get* to take action, because how we phrase things matters.
- In childhood, influential figures in your life contributed to the beliefs you have about yourself.
- Provided you aren't harming yourself, others, or the environment, do what pleases you. If it has the same effect on others, fantastic!

- Habitual thoughts produce associated beliefs, values, and feelings which impact our behaviour and the actions we take.

- The principle of manifestation is that thoughts become things, whether good or bad.

- Mindfulness makes us aware of the voices and the ability to accept their existence.

- We need a sufficient level of awareness to notice what we're saying to ourselves.

- Slowly and objectively identify the good, the bad, and the ugly of what actually happened.

- Don't try to fix the problem whilst caught up in the drama.

- Metrics matter, so measure your progress.

- We are all human. Nobody gets to demean you, especially not your mental nattering.

- People-pleasing to gain acceptance leads to resentment towards that person or yourself.

- The quality and nature of your sense of self-worth is a keystone to success.

- You're basically alright.

- Fear is our mind's way of protecting us.

Chapter One Meditation
Introducing Mindfulness Meditation

Welcome to your first mindfulness meditation created especially for *Mind Over Natter*.

We set our intention at the start of this meditation:

Try to relax into this experience, and gently reduce your expectations.

Brief Thought Prior to Meditation

It is especially good to introduce you to the first of six Meditations uniquely created for *Mind Over Natter*. As you begin your mindfulness practice for improved health, wealth, love, and happiness, I invite you to relax and let me guide you. Simply being here today is a significant contribution to your own wellbeing, so thank you for showing up.

Get comfortable. Sit with your back upright, leaning ever so slightly forward. Uncross arms and legs. Rest the back of your left hand in your right hand just in front of your naval. Touch thumbs together. Invite a sense of kindness into your awareness. Be comfortable and alert. Meditation is holding focus, not falling asleep.

Bring your attention to your shoulders. Ease the tightness in your shoulders. Let go. Become aware of your back. Stress gets trapped in the back. This can lead to back ache. Relax your back. Now, feel your neck. Imagine relaxing the tension in your neck.

Take your awareness to the breath. Observe what breathing feels like.

The body breathes in through the nose. Experience that feeling, breathing in. The belly rises as the lungs expand. A brief pause and the body naturally wants to breathe out and let go. Feel what it's like to let go.

If you lose awareness of the breath because your mind starts thinking about plans, remembering or rehashing thoughts, that's really okay. Just peacefully come back to the breath.

Follow the journey of your breath. Notice your breath as it comes in through your nostrils. Is it slightly cooler just beneath your nostrils? Trace the air moving up your nose and down into your lungs. Become aware of the air filling your lungs. See the body expand. Then, notice the contraction as the air pushes out of your lungs. Feel warm air leaving down your nose and out of your nostrils.

Observe how your whole body feels more relaxed. Bring your awareness to what relaxation feels like in our body.

Breathe in. Breathe out. Relax. Let go. If your mind is busy, mentally say: *breathing in, breathing out.*

Thoughts come up … simply let them go. Be aware of letting go. Let each thought rise and fall away. Feelings follow thoughts, so let those feelings rise and fall away. Return your awareness to your breathing. Sense the expanse of a wide-open mind and an open heart.

As we close out today's meditation, recompose the room around you. Allow the sounds of your environment to come back into your awareness, and feel yourself return fully into your body and into this space.

Our intention at the start of this meditation was to relax into this experience and to see if you could reduce your expectations. Offer some kindness to yourself for being here. This is the start of your mindfulness meditation practice as you continue to read *Mind Over Natter*.

That's it—that's meditation. All you need to do to shift from the pain and noise of your inner critics into meditation is to slow down, let go, relax, and observe the breath. When you are ready, take in a deep breath of appreciation for today's practice. We breathe in together. And we let go together—breathe out.

Take this peaceful, calm feeling with you into the world as you share the relief of letting go.

We fill our heart space with gratitude. Thank you.

May you be healthy, wealthy, loved, and happy.

CHAPTER TWO
MINDFULNESS—WHAT IS IT AND CAN I LEARN HOW TO PRACTISE IT RIGHT NOW?

"You don't have to control your thoughts;
You just have to stop letting them control you."

Soulful Reflections

Mindfulness

Mindfulness implies the mind
yet
It's heart-based, loving awareness, that
Delves deeper than thought, through cognition, beyond judgement,
Expanding ever outward by drawing ever inwards.
Breathe in, breathe out.
I'm not always there for that, for the breath that keeps me alive.
Awareness-awakened sensory explosion.
There's more than meets the eye,
Felt experience, lived emotion.
Inclusion, interaction, immersion.
Mindfulness is space
Mindfulness is spaciousness
The cessation of separation.

Understanding Mindfulness through Mindlessness.

I'm often asked, "What is mindfulness?" and one of the best ways to explain it, is to look through the lens of mindlessness.

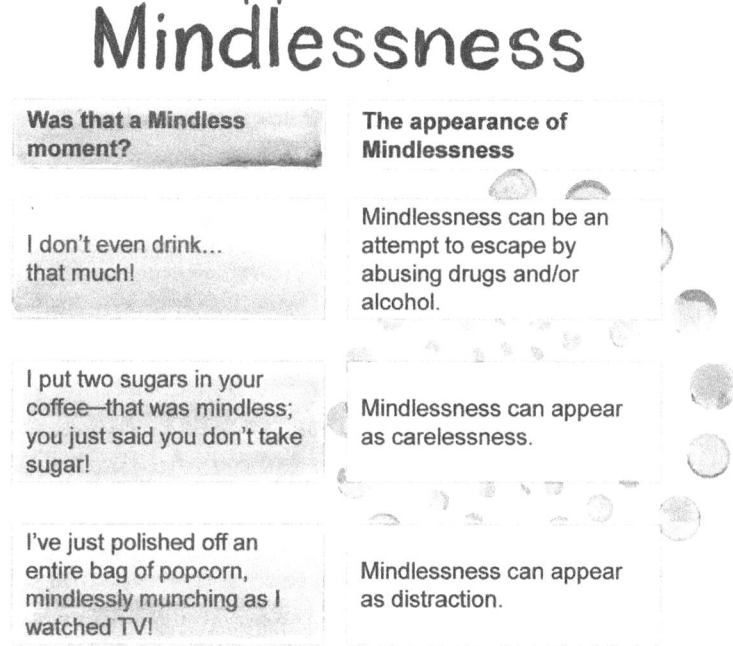

Was that a Mindless moment?	The appearance of Mindlessness
I don't even drink… that much!	Mindlessness can be an attempt to escape by abusing drugs and/or alcohol.
I put two sugars in your coffee—that was mindless; you just said you don't take sugar!	Mindlessness can appear as carelessness.
I've just polished off an entire bag of popcorn, mindlessly munching as I watched TV!	Mindlessness can appear as distraction.

Mindfulness is more than the antithesis of mindlessness. I'll continue to expand on its meaning throughout the book but for now, let's stay with mindlessness for a moment. Mindlessness isn't only about the actions we purposely take to numb out difficult experiences in life. Sometimes, our minds check out, switch off, or go blank when things get tough. Minds get muddled after a traumatic event so that when you think back, you don't have clarity about the situation. I've blocked out many phases in my life when things were difficult. There are a few more I wish I *had* blocked out because I cringe when I remember them. But that's the mind for you—sometimes it's your friend, and sometimes it's your foe.

Get Down!

I mean, it could have saved me from the memory of landing face-first, arse out on a gym mat after a failed pike. A pike in gymnastics is an extension where you reach straight arms to touch your toes. You'll often see a pike just before a tuck or a somersault. The girls in our class were squeamish about exercise, but I was new to the school and eager to please. I mistakenly thought pleasing involved prowess at sports. I hadn't been privy to the preferred methods of avoidance and criticism—two key components of high school coolness.

The girls ahead of me performed the same reluctant squirmy dance. They pressed down their skirts and exchanged knowing glances. They circled around each other and giggled about anyone who tried the trundle to the trampoline. It was meant to be a sprint, but they barely broke into a jog. They received each other with giggles into their fold when yet another of their group had deliberately sabotaged the exercise. They were eating the gym teacher alive. I couldn't believe they didn't want to simply run a bit, bounce a bit, and at least pretend to reach for a toe touch and then land. It seemed like fun to me. I was actually quite eager to give it a go. Some of the excluded girls at least tried to run and spring off the trampoline, but we all saw how they held back. It didn't win them any points with the cool girls, and they quickly faded into anonymity without drawing attention to themselves.

Teenage boys and girls of two combined classes filled the gymnasium. The boys were on one side of the floor out-testosteroning each other with skills on the rings and the pommel horse. They gawked at the girls and hoped the girls were gawking back. It got very noisy and the smell of sockless feet combined with nervous sweat was so pungent, I was reluctant to breathe.

It was my turn next. I blazed toward the trampoline. Maybe the cool girls simply *couldn't* do it, but they played it off as though they *wouldn't* do it. Maybe they'd be impressed with someone bold enough to blast off as I did. I wanted their approval, maybe even to show the boys I was as strong as they were. I admit I was also keen to reward the teacher with at least one pupil who'd been inspired.

I set off on a sprint so swift I nearly overshot the trampoline. If I'd had any more boost on my bounce, I'd probably have launched right into the ceiling. Propelled skyward, I was up, up, and away. I heard the silence domino beneath me, one after another—nerds, boys, and girls. The knock-on effect of jaw-dropping silence seemed to prolong my flight.

My previous all-girls school had been competitive. We tore around the gym circuits there like we were Olympians. We didn't bother wearing anything under our skirts, except our panties. What I didn't know, as my arse dangled precariously above the staring crowd, was that at a co-ed school, it was inconceivable for a girl to wear any kind of sports skirt without bike shorts underneath. I knew I'd already branded myself with whatever loser name they'd inflict on me, so I didn't bother to complete the pike. My decision wasn't all defeatist. I quickly became aware of my next imminent danger, specifically that I was hurtling past the landing mat. *Get down!* my inner critics shouted.

Gravity brought me back to earth faster than I expected. Gone was the casual land and stride off the mat I'd envisioned. Gone was any hope of acceptance. Splat. I landed face first, arse second, skirt third. My skirt flapped itself up my back and exposed the journey my panties had made right up my crack. My arse cheeks laid bare in a still-convulsing cellulite wobble when the last gasp sounded. I'll never know if there was anything salvable at that stage, but my next move entirely sealed my fate. This is the part that I wish my mind *would* have blanked out, the part where I stood up on the mat and bowed with an added arm flurry. The leader of the cool girls burst out laughing, and her gang obediently followed, smashing the silence into a cacophony of mocking. Everyone, even the nerds, the teacher, and those who hadn't even seen the mangled mess I'd made of myself laughed in derision.

Sometimes painful experiences imbed vivid details that fuel regret. I've spent years torturing myself with regret, shame and guilt. If you've punished yourself too, I urge you to stay present with what's happening right now. If I insist on remembering something but I can't quite recollect it this minute, I risk inviting my inner critics to stampede in with judgments about my *sieve for brains,* and it isn't long before I feel stressed and anxious. Mindfulness reminds me to reconnect with my mind and body which allows me to be present in the current moment. An excellent way to meander away from mindfulness into mindlessness is to get stuck in memories or bogged down by plans. It is easy to become distracted and removed from the experience of the present. We can build focus through mindfulness. It takes consistency and practice.

The monk attributed with bringing mindfulness meditation and a great calming wave to the West is Vietnamese Buddhist Master, poet, writer, speaker, peace activist, founder of the Plum Village Monastery (six monasteries altogether around the world), Thich Nhat Hanh. There are millions of mindfulness practitioners around the world who've embraced mindfulness meditation through his loving kindness, the compassionate way he leads his life, and the fine example he sets of what it is to immerse in benevolence and understanding, and how to extend that to others. In "The Art of Living," he expands on mindfulness and how we can learn to live in the present moment, reconnecting our body and mind.

> Our body is there, but our mind is somewhere else, not with the body. Our mind is alienated from the body. It is with our projects, our worries, our fears. We can work on a computer for hours and completely forget our body, until something starts to hurt. But how can we say we are truly living our life if we've forgotten we have a body? If our mind is not with our body, we cannot say that we are fully present. We cannot say that we're truly alive. [1]

Thich Nhat Hanh communicates in a soft, measured voice. No matter which format: written, audio or video, I sense his gentle demeanour, and it calms me. He says something so simple and yet so poignant during meditation, "Enjoy." When you're mindfully aware of the breath in meditation, it's true—it's a most enjoyable experience. The mind doesn't always have enjoyable memories or insights to share with us. We know the mind doesn't really forget anything. It's constantly absorbing information and storing or deleting it, depending on how it perceives the relevance of any given moment. I suggest you take control of your mind. Instead of letting it decide what you want to retain or discard, become conscious of what's going on around you, and perhaps more pertinently, what's going on inside you. If you think you aren't generally a mindless person, you might find some familiarity in some of the scenarios shared by my clients about the times they noticed their mindlessness.

Can you recognise yourself in any of these scenarios?

1 point = Not really, no (not often)
2 points = Often enough (regularly)
3 points = Are you kidding? I have the t-shirt! (frequently)

Scenario	Not really, no	Often enough	I have the t-shirt
You park the car and suddenly realise it's the first time you've been present for the whole drive. How did you get there? What happened in the traffic?			
You walk past a building that's been there for over a year and wonder, "When did they do that?"			
You've been binge-watching your favourite show and you realise someone must have binged on the bag of crisps next to you on the couch! Was that someone you?			
Ever read a paragraph or maybe even a whole page of a book and wondered what the heck was happening because your eyes read the text, but your mind didn't?			
What about walking into a sign, a person, a door - anything because you were on your phone and not aware of your surroundings?			
Been working at the computer or gaming and suddenly realize you've been bursting for the loo for hours?			
How about being in a daydream (either memory, worrying, or planning), and someone asks you a question that you clearly have no idea how to answer?			
What about walking into a room and suddenly realising you have no idea what you went there to do?			
Misplaced or lost anything?			
Said something that you didn't intend to be hurtful but the effect was deeply wounding to someone else?			
Forgotten something you needed at school, work, gym, on holiday?			
Nearly driven up someone's rear end because they braked and you weren't watching?			
Faked knowing who you were speaking to, or you knew them, but had forgotten their name?			
TOTAL SCORE			

Scenarios measuring mindlessness.

How did you do? The higher the score, the more frequent your experience of mindlessness.

If you aren't in control of your mind and directing its focus, your past controls it from previous experience which then conditions your future. This haze of existence exacerbates our busy lives, which leads to more stress and anxiety. So, what can we do about it? Jon Kabat-Zinn explains how mindfulness can counteract those difficult feelings. "Mindfulness is about love and loving life. When you cultivate this love, it gives you clarity and compassion for life and your actions happen in accordance with that."

In 1979, Jon Kabat-Zinn recruited chronically-ill patients who weren't responding well to traditional treatments to participate in his newly formed eight-week stress-reduction program, which is called Mindfulness-Based Stress Reduction (MBSR). Substantial research has demonstrated how mindfulness-based interventions improve mental and physical health.

Jon Kabat-Zinn has made mindfulness accessible to many Westerners and is often referenced for his heartfelt definitions of the practice. He says, "I pair the heart and mind together deliberately since that's possibly the most effective way of describing the experience of mindfulness—it is wholehearted awareness of the present moment. In "Falling Awake," he expands,

> Luckily, if we miss the moment because we are distracted by one thing or another, caught up in thinking or in our emotions, or with the busyness of what always seems to need getting done, there is always the next moment to begin again, to stop and drop into wakefulness in this moment of now. [2]

Listening in

What's your inner voice been saying so far? It might be ranting and protesting, or it might be pretending it's not that bad. To get a real-time assessment so I could accurately describe what my mind sounds like, I played detective. Here's a peek.

My aim was to determine what my inner voices say, how they carry messages, and what impact they make on my thoughts, feelings, and behaviours. Our inner dialogue starts cracking the whip the moment we wake. My first thought was more of a fright than a full-blown thought. It was an unconscious reaction. My phone alarm ship-horned me out of a dream. In terror, I simultaneously levitated and thwacked at the phone to stop the blasts. *I really need to get a new alarm,* I thought, but was interrupted by the retort of my inner critics:

You ALWAYS say that.
Famous last words.
You're no good at tech.

How did I feel after that negative barrage only a few seconds into the day? Awful. I bent down to pick up my phone, which had crashed to the floor in a screen-cracking kind of way. Thankfully, it was fine. *That's a relief,* I thought as I cradled it. The next inner critic agreed, *Thank goodness for that screen protector.* "Kid Kane," my inner child, felt safe to join since this voice seemed kinder, *And I really love the cover. That's my favourite colour!* My practical inner adult nodded, *It's effective and wasn't that expensive.* Unfortunately, the mere thought of money evoked poverty consciousness, which sucked me into a tunnel of financial anxiety. Overwhelm set in soon after, crowding my mind with how much I had to do today, how much I didn't get done yesterday, and then a lecture on how I should be more mindful. As a mindfulness practitioner, I really ought to be in better control of my thoughts and feelings. Slap!

In the shower, I noticed stress rising up and physically impacting my body. When I inquired further, I was surprised to find my inner critic was uncomfortable because my shampoo wasn't at the same level as my conditioner. *Really?* I almost laughed. *Does it matter if the two aren't in synch? I'm sure this happens to most people.* My inner critic wouldn't let it go, *Well, perhaps when you get the next set, you could be more mindful and measure out the exact amount from each bottle.*

Listen in to your inner voices. As you've been reading these examples, did any of your voices agree or dispute what mine said? It's fascinating to actively listen rather than just absorbing everything the inner voices say. Take it a level further. Filter your observation through compassion. With kindness, notice thoughts. We're so used to reacting to thoughts and taking them at face value. It's liberating to step into the role of a witness merely viewing thoughts. With mindfulness, you can grow the gap between the thought as it arises and how you respond to it.

Mindfulness

To understand mindfulness is to recognize we're mindless most of the time. We operate on autopilot, reacting, blaming others, and getting caught up in anxiety. We're not really present in our lives. We're hardly present for our kids, even when we get home. How many of us drag our wounds from past relationships into the next one? Most of us drive mindlessly. We eat mindlessly. Life before mindfulness was like a pinball machine. I was the ball, bouncing off everything, getting paddled and whacked off course. In the end, nothing could stop me from falling down the hole and disappearing from myself. Mindfulness is for everyone—all demographics, all ages, all orientations. Kids can even learn it. It's for teens, senior citizens, colleagues, and couples caught up in conflict. Even if you doubt it, you've already sampled moments of mindfulness.

Mindfulness describes a method of thinking and noticing—of multisensory awareness. Mindfulness refers to the act of contemplating thoughts. There are many aspects of mindfulness, but some useful areas include:

- Meditation
- Relaxation
- Therapy

- Introspection, non-judgmental self-observation
- Becoming aware of our thoughts, developing an inquiry about them
- The qualities of thinking that lead towards calm, peace, and happiness
- Awareness of negative thoughts and behaviours that detrimentally impact our lives and those around us
- Compassion including self-compassion
- Resilience
- Forgiveness
- Self-worth, self-confidence
- Lifestyle, community, planetary issues

Do I Have to Convert to Buddhism to Practice Mindfulness?

I participated in a 30-Day wellness challenge recently, and we were sharing tips and tricks on social media. The group made considerable health gains, and we were uploading motivational memes and videos to keep us inspired as the challenge ended. One of the ladies launched an unexpected attack on some of the affirming memes saying they contradicted her religious views. I was surprised at her visceral protest and then wondered what kind of religion was so intolerant of something that was warm, loving, and kind? The short answer is no; you don't have to be a Buddhist to practice mindfulness.

Mindfulness is an ancient practice, older than but expanded through Buddhism, which offers many teachings on personal improvement and self-development. These are accessible from a secular viewpoint. The conversion that *Mind Over Natter* promotes is that you overcome your negative inner critics and transform your life from calamity to clarity. Often, we have strong opinions about spiritual practices different from our own, and yet we have no knowledge about them. We tend to label, box, pigeon hole for our perceived safety. Perhaps there is a unifying energy for good than our sense of separateness would allow us to believe. In "Living Buddha, Living Christ," Zen Master, Thich Nhat Hanh, spends an entire book showing unity across faiths.

> "To me, mindfulness is very much like the Holy Spirit. Both are agents of healing. When you have mindfulness, you have love and understanding, you see more deeply, and you can heal wounds in your own mind. The Buddha was called the King of Healers. In the Bible, when someone touches Christ, he or she is healed. It is not just touching a cloth that brings the miracle. When you touch deep understanding and love, you are healed." [3]

I do believe there's a higher power, a Mother Father Creator, Love. I wouldn't want to live without the spiritual support and healing of that benevolence, loving kindness, and encouragement. What you believe is your choice, and I leave that for you to determine. I want to help you as much as I can, and I hope that mindfulness will *underline,* not *undermine* your faith.

Mindfulness Is an Experience Rather Than a Concept.

Although we use the word *mind*, since the entry point is through the mind, it is often described as *heartfulness* or *kindfulness*. Does that seem a*iry-fairy,* *head-in-the-clouds*? Were those your thoughts or your inner critic's judgments? Inner critics are constantly buzzing, even when we think we have them pointed in a single direction. Sometimes, we need to rescue our awareness from the crevice into which they crash our thoughts. Maybe phrases like, *heartfelt* or *being kind* feel more appealing.

Emanant mindfulness teacher and Psychologist, Dr Tara Brach says, "Kindness will change your biology." When did we buy into the idea that being kind was for sissies? What's wrong with compassion and caring? More to the point, isn't that *precisely* what's wrong with the world? We've lost contact with tenderness. We're so hotly pursuing our worldly ambitions we've forgotten that we're the ones who have to live in the world we create. *Heartfulness* and *kindfulness* lead us into a broader appreciation of mindfulness—it's a space we create for ourselves that starts in our minds, is experienced in our hearts, and expands through our senses, deepening into our whole being.

Want to try it? Let's give it a go right now.

Exercise: Experience mindfulness in one minute.

Bring your awareness to your thoughts. Leave the external world for a moment, and notice what's going on in your thoughts. Sometimes, thoughts form resistance, so you might hear the inner critics complaining one after the other:

> *No, this is stupid.*
> *It's not for me.*
> *Who cares?*
> *I don't have time for this.*
> *Oh, hell if this is an interactive book. I'm outta here.*
> *Can I do this later? I want the information first.*

Shepherd your awareness back to the present moment. Try not to rehearse plans about the future or rehash regrets from the past. Simply be present in this moment right here, right now. Read the guidance of the meditation out loud and then experience what it says to do.

Our minute starts now.

Breathe in. Breathe out.
Move passed the mind's thoughts.
Feel your body.
Scan your senses: what can you see, hear, taste, touch, smell?
Notice your breath.
How do you feel physically and emotionally?
Now let go of feeling, emotion, senses and thoughts and return your attention to the breath.
Breathe in. Breathe out.

That's it—the start of mindfulness in a minute.

Mindfulness practice embodies several attitudes but as an introduction, I'll list eight as suggested by Former Monk and Mindfulness Meditation teacher, Sean Fargo. These attitudes contribute to the growth and flourishing of your mind, heart and body.

1. **Learner's Mind** – Seeing things as a visitor in a foreign land, everything is new and curious.

2. **Non-judgmental** – Becoming impartial, without any labels of right or wrong or good or bad. It is simply allowing things to be.

3. **Acknowledgment** – Recognizing things as they are.

4. **Settled** – Being comfortable in the moment and content where you are.

5. **Composed** – Being calm and in control with compassion and insight.

6. **Letting be** – Letting things be as they are with no need to change them.

7. **Self-reliant** – Deciding on your own, from your own experiences, what's true or not.

8. **Self-compassionate** – Loving yourself as you are with no criticism or self-reproach." [4]

Learner's Mind is often referred to as Beginner's Mind. As you read, even though you've heard all this before, bring a Beginner's Mind to *Mind Over Natter*. This inquisitive intention slows the inner critics from telling you they know everything, and it gives you a chance to learn something or more fully understand with clarity. Bring your awareness inward. Mindfulness is about awareness—not answers.

Inner critics become anxious because they assume you're trying to clear your mind of all thought. Not even the most dedicated can achieve total emptiness. Be softer with your expectations. It's less about doing and more about simply being. Slow down, give yourself time. You don't even have to dismiss the critics, just move into an energy of acknowledging, accepting, and allowing.

Inner Voices Are Nattering All the Time

Inner voices speak in a variety of tones, and each has their own objective. When you couple intention with awareness, it's a helpful technique to step out of the inner-critic trance. See yourself watching your thought process—the act of witnessing the thoughts rather than being subjected to their effects. This calms anxiety. As you practice this observational mode, you can begin to distance yourself. You might think, *Oh, isn't that interesting? My mind was thinking anxious thoughts?* As a witness to your thoughts, you restore authority to your mind and its ability to change. By becoming conscious of your consciousness, you are no longer hypnotised by the anxiety, anger, fear, or stress the inner critics evoke.

Most of what we think, say, and do is habitual. Since these programmes run automatically and unconsciously, we seldom think to question their accuracy or refresh and update them. Left on repeat, they become self-fulfilling prophecies.

How a Thought Becomes a Self-Fulfilling Prophecy

Thought + Feeling = Effect = Act = Thought + Feeling = Effect = Act, repeat.

This gets interesting when you layer in beliefs between thoughts and feelings.

Thought + Belief + Feeling = Effect = Act = Thought + Belief + Feeling = Effect = Act, repeat.

A belief doesn't necessarily have to be true—it's merely a habitually recycled thought. Our beliefs sit in our subconscious, and for many of us they remain without any investigation as to their validity, accuracy, or justifiability. It's important to know what your internal beliefs are because knowing them can help you clear the clutter, get you out of our own way, so that you can align with your desires. We don't have to keep on believing our beliefs—it's possible to discard those that no longer work.

Worrying Is a Habit

I still slump into worry every now and then. If I'm not mindful, worry converts to anxiety, and then it takes much more effort to pull myself out of that state. It takes awareness to notice when we're yielding to anxious thoughts. Excessive worrying is common. We mindlessly fan the flames of worry even though we know it won't stop things from happening. Worry won't make the bad things stop. In fact, it creates an atmosphere for them to get worse. More pertinently, worry blocks our awareness from seeing the good around us. If we want less worry and more peace, we have to minimize our worrisome thoughts and maximize our cultivation of happy thoughts. Expansive habits can equally create self-fulfilling scenarios. Instead of dreading the worst, train yourself to anticipate the best. Get a single-pointed focus on your preferred outcomes.

 ## Meditation—Thoughts Are like Clouds

Thoughts are elusive. If you try and grab them, they escape, and float out of your awareness just as ethereally as they floated in. Conjure an image of clouds. Did you imagine actual clouds or pictures of clouds? Whatever visual you created, see if you can hold the image. The idea is that you don't have to analyse, criticise, understand, be fearful of, or judge the clouds—simply notice them. Are the clouds set against a blue-sky, or are there more grey clouds behind them? Can you tell if the clouds are moving swiftly or imperceptibly? Are they in the upper atmosphere, or do they feel close? Are the clouds white and fluffy or grey and ominous?

In the same way, try not to be too cognitive about your thoughts—allow them to float in and float away.

Gradually, the critics within will slow down. When they do, you can sink deeper into a state of relaxation—a kinder space of awareness. When the gaps between thoughts widen, become aware of your breath. Notice the breath as you inhale. Feel the body expand as air begins to fill the lungs, then release the air. Let go. Just like you experienced mindfulness in a minute, this is all it takes to ease into meditation.

Meditation in a Moment

Meditation helps to set aside what's going on externally and within the mind. It brings awareness to the body. Be fully present with the sensations happening within your body. Then, deeper still, drop into your emotions, and be aware of how you are feeling right now. Being aware of your feelings gives you the power to change them. In this short time, you've already been meditating. It's a simple practice, but it's not easy.

Once you experience the tranquillity of a calmer mind where your thoughts have slowed down, you can begin to appreciate how frenetic your mind is when it's left to its own devices.

There's an incessant commentary of everything we think, feel, and do, which exacerbates our feelings of frustration, hopelessness, stress, and fatigue. Inner critics constantly natter about external circumstances. Not only do we suffer negative limiting beliefs about not being good enough, we also condemn our thoughts for not being good enough. Sometimes, we worry we aren't being mindful or meditating correctly. Being judged by the inner critics adds to our stress. Why? They inflict a second injury with their negativity! We feel bad and then feel worse by judging ourselves for that feeling. Mindfulness isn't about deleting negative thoughts—it's about noticing them, accepting them as they are, and then being aware that just like clouds, they can dissolve away.

If you've made previous attempts at mindfulness meditation, you might observe your negative inner critic refusing to affirm your return to the practice. Instead, it berates you for not sticking to your commitment in the first place. There's no pleasing some critics. The positive voices will remind you that mindfulness isn't an achievement; it's a way of being. Lean towards the quiet of non-judgmental moment-to-moment awareness. Your senses provide an excellent gateway to the peace of mind meditation offers. By tuning in to your senses at the start of meditation, you move out of you head, away from thought and into the body, and then, into experience. Once you stop clinging to thought, you will begin to embrace calm, and when that happens, you can gently release your awareness of sight, sound, smell, taste, and touch. Then, you can drift into tranquil silence.

Meditation is an expansion of mindfulness. It's a deep experience of awareness. Meditation helps to differentiate between thought and the inner critic's opinion about thought. Have you ever asked for directions, but worried you'd get lost, (or doubted they knew the way), you stop listening and now you don't know if it was left or right at the stop street? Many of us forget people's names at functions because we didn't really hear them in the first place (our critics were complaining so loudly about how much they hate networking). Whenever I'm learning the rules of a new game, or taking an instruction, I try to lower the volume of my nattering inner critics so I can listen mindfully. It doesn't always work. Sometimes, I jump the gun, and leap prematurely into action.

Spray It Again, Sam

I had to have a barium meal to determine why I choke. The nurse held up two plastic medical cups, one smaller than the other. "This one is bicarbonate of soda, and this one is lemon juice," she explained. I was about to tip the powder into the lemon juice, shooter style, when she cautioned, "You pop the bicarb in your mouth first, and then keep your mouth open and add the lemon juice." All I heard was, *keep your mouth open,* so I chucked the bicarb into my open mouth and added the lemon juice. Frothy bubbles burst out of my mouth, fizzled over my face, onto my chest, and sputtered down my right arm. Just when I thought it couldn't get worse, I growled out a gassy burp. The nurse, her assistant, and the doctor stood behind the X-Ray screen, flabbergasted. I apologised, and as I tried to stifle more emerging burps, I started coughing – and couldn't stop! I was coughing, spluttering, and apologising all at the same time.

Had I been more mindful, I'd have gently placed the bicarb on my tongue, added the lemon juice, and swallowed the fizziness with a closed mouth. I pre-empted the instruction, and moved directly into action, not fully clarifying what was expected. Then, it started—their bombardment. My inner critics condemned me for being stupid and too fat as I stood, arse hanging out of the medical gown that didn't close at the back. My critics continued to chastise, and my inner child wanted to cry.

The lemony bicarb bubbles popped and soaked my gown in a sticky, cold mess, and the nurse had to tell me twice to turn to my left and turn to my right for the X-Ray because I hadn't heard her instruction beyond the noise in my head.

I'm thankful for the reprieve I get from my inner critics when I entrust myself to meditation even though they land some lashings at the start of each meditation. They might even have some intermittent resurgence during the practice, but thankfully, I can quell the nattering and enjoy noticing other things. That's intrinsic to the art of mindfulness—noticing, awareness, and non-judgement.

When meditating, there's no need to change thoughts or feelings, merely acknowledge them in the moment. There isn't a dictate as to what's right or wrong in meditation. There's a serene, tranquil, quietness that seems to emerge from the heart, relaxing the body. The quiet is kind, gentle, intimate, and deeply soothing. I feel comforted, loved, and safe. If you could experience this sense of belonging and know you aren't alone, you are deeply cared for, you are respected, and you are valued, I'm sure you'd be inspired to try meditation. You are a priceless piece of the puzzle; the world is not the same when you are disconnected from what makes you happy. Your happiness and sense of wellbeing are vital to the completed picture.

Since meditation and mindfulness are experiential, the best is for you to sit in formal practice. If you can join a group meditation, I encourage you to do so as this will enhance your experience, especially if you are a beginner. You might meet some amazing people. We're better when we connect than when we isolate ourselves. When social distancing, I've led and participated in numerous meditation sessions online in the comfort of my own home. The meditations in this book are offered as a multi-sensory experience with words, sounds, and visuals. If you like, record the meditations in your voice. The more you practice, the more you will notice the benefits of meditation in your life and how it creates space for you to understand who you are and what you want. You will enjoy better relationships (including the one you have with yourself), an increase in confidence, a sense of happiness, and enhanced resilience. Perhaps you'll start giving nutrition more attention and become more active, embrace new experiences, sleep better, and begin to enjoy your own company.

Be Bright, Be Brief, and Be Mindful

- Our inner dialogue starts nattering the moment we wake.
- Inner voices impact our thoughts, feelings, and behaviours.
- Filter your observation through compassion.
- To understand mindfulness is to recognise we're mindless most of the time.
- We operate on autopilot—reacting, blaming others, and getting caught up in anxiety.
- Mindfulness is for everyone—all demographics, all ages, all orientations.
- Mindfulness is not about answers but awareness.
- Move into an energy of acknowledging, accepting, and allowing.
- Worrying won't make the bad things stop, in fact, it creates an atmosphere for them to get worse.
- Instead of dreading the worst that could happen, start anticipating the best that could happen.
- Mindfulness isn't changing negative thoughts; it's noticing them, accepting them as they are, and being aware that just like clouds, they can drift away.
- Meditation is an expansion of mindfulness.
- Intrinsic to the art of mindfulness is noticing, being aware, and non-judgment.

- With mindfulness, enjoy better relationships (including the one you have with yourself), increased confidence, enhanced resilience, and a sense of happiness. Perhaps you'll start giving nutrition more attention and become more active, embrace new experiences, sleep better, begin to enjoy your own company.
- There's no right or wrong way to practise mindfulness.

Chapter Two Meditation
Mindfulness—What Is It and Can I Learn How to
Practise It Right Now?

Welcome to your next mindfulness meditation created especially for *Mind Over Natter*.

We set our intention at the start of this meditation:

- To allow our thoughts to come up just like clouds in a sky.

Brief Thought Prior to Meditation

Thoughts come up. It's possible to soften the negative self-talk that fuels thoughts. Sometimes, the inner critic can be cruel and harsh. The inner criticism may be unreasonable and even untrue, but nevertheless, we find it difficult to escape the pain it causes us. Your inner critic may say you aren't okay. It might even doubt you've ever been okay or could ever be okay, but we're here and breathing, and that's okay!

We're gently easing ourselves into the place where we can take a moment to be present and enjoy our practice. Allow the sounds in your immediate environment to fade further away and permit yourself to let go and deeply relax.

Get comfortable. If you're new to meditation practice, simply do what feels natural for you. Uncross arms and legs. If you practice regularly, seated on a cushion or a chair, take up your meditation posture. Back straight. Left hand in your right hand. Touch thumbs.

Give yourself time to settle.

Become aware of your breath.

Breathe in through the nose. Experience that feeling—breathing in. Your belly rises as the lungs expand. A brief pause and your body naturally wants to breathe out and let go. Relax. Take your awareness deeper as you follow the breath.

Breathe for a few moments. Allow yourself time to transition from the activities of the day into the quiet of this meditation.

Picture your mind as a sky with thoughts floating across your awareness like clouds. We're not trying to disperse the thoughts, but be curious about the thoughts. You might think, *Isn't that interesting, I came to meditate and my thoughts are like storm clouds full of anxiety?* It won't be long before that thought drifts away. Your mind is like an expansive sky. There's so much open space in your expanding mind.

Thoughts drift into your awareness like clouds. Simply let them go. Feelings follow thoughts, so let those feelings come up, and then let them go. Feel relaxed as you see the clouds of your mind appear and disappear. You don't have to get too involved in your thoughts.

Rest here in the expanse of your mind as thoughts and feelings drift in and out like clouds.

As we close today's meditation, recompose the room around you. Allow the sounds of your environment to come back into your awareness, and feel yourself return fully into your body and into your space.

When you're ready, take in a deep breath of appreciation for today's practice. We breathe together—breathe in. And we let go together—breathe out.

Take this peaceful, calm feeling with you into the world as you enjoy the relief of letting go.

We fill our heart space with gratitude. Thank you.

May you be healthy, wealthy, loved, and happy.

CHAPTER THREE
MINDLESSNESS—MY LIFE'S A MESS. WHAT CAN I DO ABOUT IT?

"We either own our stories or they own us. Only when we have the courage to own our history are we able to write a brave new ending to our story."

Brené Brown

No More

Slithering...
  ...Sliding...
 ...Slinking
   ...Sneaking...
       ...Skulking...
    ...Side-winding
Mind-sidling.
Disguised as the voice of reason,
The incessant whisper that
Infiltrates, insinuates, alludes then eludes.
A persistent, prompting, poison that
Suggests, rescinds, escalates then rebukes.
How sly the venomous assimilation.
Cruel corruptor of courage, if not twisting and turning, then a
contaminating contagion.
Your suffocating grasp,
Crushes my hope.
Your toxic intrusion,
Destroys my joy.
Whisper no more.
Let loose your grip!
Slide away—your slithering subversion laid bare.
For in my breath I've learned that the true voice stands clear,
And drawing me close,
Through quiet convalescence,
I find
My life, my life
This is MY life

When Life's a Mess Because of Mindlessness

The "No More" poem refers to the serpentine nature of some of my destructive inner critics: sometimes they suffocate and sometimes they poison. In a state of mindlessness, our inner critics hiss and curse at us, poisoning our minds. Without a gatekeeper, negative inner critics can inflict as much damage as they like. When we live mindlessly, we allow our negative inner critics to slither around our thoughts, beliefs, and feelings, making us victims! It's imperative you *hear* what they're saying, then challenge and refute them. If some of the nattering has value, then fantastic—but don't be overpowered by the negative and often limiting, untrue messages because those nattering's will cause you pain!

The good news is that we can stop perpetuating the pain by addressing the source of our pain. It takes a single thought to notice you're not happy, and, if mindful, have the intention to do something about it. Begin an overhaul of your life, one breath at a time.

- feeling victimized. *Why me?*
- feeling bewildered. *What just happened?* Or *Where did that come from?*
- feeling angry. *Fuck you! Fuck that! And fuck this especially!*
- feeling vengeful. *I'll show them what pain looks like.*
- feeling full of blame. *It's not my fault, you did this to me!*
- feeling indignant. *Do they know who I am?*

What can we do about pain in our lives? The first step is becoming aware. Aware of *why* we feel pain, aware of *where* that pain manifests in our body, aware of the negative beliefs that caused the pain in the first place.

Instead of getting caught up in the pain, it is massively empowering to enter into a pain paradox: gain distance from pain by leaning into it. Don't identify with the pain, identify where it is: physically, emotionally, mentally etc. If we don't become mindful, we get stuck in a self-perpetuating pattern of pain, harm, and exposure to the same scenarios that caused the pain.

In return, we experience more pain so it continues. It seems so logical when we describe it like this, yet each of us has been stuck in a rut at some stage in our lives. Develop an observational stance. Look at the situation with compassion. By expanding the quality of our attention, we not only pause the scene, but we can also choose to look in another direction. How many of us are used to scrambling from one saga to another? There's too much going on, too many balls in the air—it's inevitable that one or more will drop. Shift perspective—think as a coach planning some moves rather than as a drama queen who collapses into a heap when things go wrong.

Take AIM
Attention + Intention + Mindfulness

Mindlessness Crumbles in the Face of Planning

Mindlessness is avoidable!

Start planning and designing strategies rather than reacting and clamouring. Integrate some play into your designs. Get creative and enjoy noticing how you are getting on top of the negative inner critics' strategies. The more mindful you become of their tactics, the better you can predict them and change your tactics to achieve your preferred outcomes.

Planning will support your efforts to be more effective. Bumble along as before, risking stress, mistakes and accidents, or implement the night before and plan daily for clarity and resilience.

Plan the night before:

a) Appropriate nutrition and rest the night before.

b) Setting your intention to rest well and to expect a good outcome from your day.

c) Meditate (Yoga Nidra) or do a body scan for relaxation into sleep.

d) Wardrobe: Plan it, prep it, test it. Have it ready for the morning, and dress for success. Best thing you can wear, is a smile.

e) Transport: If you have a meeting and it's at a new location, Google Map it to see where it is in relation to your home or office. Look at the satellite view too. Sometimes, doing a test run is helpful. Choose best mode of transport, and have the relevant tickets, parking instructions, routes, fuel, and a backup handwritten note of directions in case your phone dies or there isn't signal. Know how much time you'll need, then give yourself an extra fifteen minutes.

f) Mindful breathing: take three mindful breaths as you're prepping.

g) Tech: Pack what you need, like the relevant chargers, etc.

h) Have a note pad and pen beside your bed if you wake up and need to remember something. Write it down and then let your mind relax. You've got this. Sleep well.

The Top Ten Daily Plan

1. As soon as you wake up, direct your mind to gratitude.

2. In the morning, have an outline of the flow of the day in terms of time, deliverables, meetings, etc. Before the day gets going, write Morning Pages (from Julia Cameron, "The Artist's Way," three foolscap pages of free-flowing stream of consciousness writing) then meditate, stretch, move your body (at home or at the gym), hydrate, eat intuitively, and mindfully.

3. Stay mindful, do a meditation. Be present, breathe mindfully during the day, and do as many little physical exercises as you can—walk, lunge, ab crunches, arm lifts, calf raises, rotate your shoulders, etc.

4. Intend to be patient: When things come up to test your patience, (and they will—calamity operating under Murphy's Law dictates it.) smile, and be glad you are prepped and ready. Notice how much easier it is to get through challenges with mindfulness rather than raging against them in mindlessness.

5. Perform an act of kindness for someone (they don't need to know it was you).

6. Tune in to the positive mental critics. Encourage the positive voices to keep reassuring you that you are basically alright. Realign if you shift into a negative mood.

Breeze along with a feeling of gratitude. Whenever you can drop your attention into your heart, send compassion to yourself for getting through the day and to others for the same.

7. Sounds: Play your feel-good tunes.

8. Happy Cues: Laughter Yoga, do a minute of gentle laughing for no reason. Volunteer the laughter at first and see if it spills into spontaneous laughter. Watch a happy video and/or read something that lights you up inside.

9. Daily Affirmation: If you have the time and inclination, develop an affirmation for the day, and say it as often as possible, something like, "I've got this."

10. Choosing Joy: Enjoy the day even if the tasks aren't enjoyable. It's *your* life and you only have this day, so choose to find or create enjoyment as you go along.

*Mindfulness is a practice
that requires consistency
but its dividends pay off immediately
and increase incrementally
as you advance into higher
states of awareness.*

#mindovernatterbook

Mindfulness helps us realise we created some of the disasters in our lives. If you want to sustain a suffering mind, live in mindlessness. If you want a better day every day, become more mindful, and use the simplicity of planning to create clarity from calamity.

The Breath of Life

We are mostly mindless about the breath - the very thing that's key to keeping us alive! Have you ever been so acutely focused on tasks you realise you're holding your breath? If I catch a fright, I'll gasp and then forget to breathe. What about aerobic exercise and those deep breaths needed to fuel our muscles? In deep relaxation, our breathing slows down.

Breathing can range from refined and delicate to heaving and desperate. Our thoughts can even impact breathing. Just thinking about something scary causes us to shallow breathe. Many of us are locked in a cycle of stress, and our breathing follows the pattern. Breathing is automatic, which is a good thing, because many of us are so busy trying to multi-task, we might forget about it if it were up to us.

Top tip:
Multi-tasking is mindlessness.
It causes exhaustion
and muddles the mind.
Do less of it, and you'll feel better.
Focus on one thing at a time.

#mindovernatterbook

Mindful breathing is dropping into observational breath awareness. Just like the meditation of thoughts as clouds, we can't seem to hold our attention exclusively on the breath since thoughts drift in and out of our awareness. That's okay. It's a fascinating meditation to observe how quickly you lose track of the breath before distractions set in. It's worthwhile to drop in and see how your body is breathing—at work, in the car, after lunch, etc. Notice your breath whenever you can - it's actually the key to shifting you out of mindlessness. That simple choice to check in on your breath puts you into a state of mindfulness.

Using the Breath to Step Clear of Mindlessness

How about a check-in right now?

How is your breathing?

Inhale. Exhale. Notice with your next breath what it feels like to breathe in and say in your mind, *I am breathing in.* Then, exhale and say, *I am breathing out.*

Breathing is the easiest way to calm ourselves. Life gets busy and stressful. A single breath can help disarm anxiety before it takes hold. Even if a crisis erupts, the habit of taking three deep breaths will calm and help you see more clearly before you even respond. "Just breathe," as people say when things get tough.

Developing self-compassion is one of the most important aspects for you to master as you return to mindful living!

Many of us measure our self-worth against our net-worth. When we lose a job or a relationship, we find it difficult to validate ourselves. We pack on additional stress by trying to live up to false expectations. It's not just our stress that's exhausting—what about that friend who's never happy and everything's wrong? You don't dare ask how they are for fear of being sucked into their drama. They lay it on thick and you leave the conversation feeling drained, like your joy was just mood-hoovered out of you. You don't have to solve everyone's problems and mindful breathing will prevent you from being a problem for others.

How to Handle the Cruel Inner Critic

Our inner critics hide in plain sight, so it is easier to spot them than you might think. It never occurred to me that I wasn't the thoughts I was thinking. I had never conceived that the beliefs I upheld weren't necessarily true, or even more frightening, who would I be if those beliefs weren't true? This questioning paralysed me in fear. Fear is sneaky that way, it slithers in and infiltrates under the guise of a voice of reason. It assimilates into your thoughts and with each fearful permutation it suggests—by means of the nattering in your mind—you are increasingly more trapped and unable to escape its coils. It was suffocating me. In addition to the terror, my ego was ashamed. I was in full victim mode, and I had to get out.

In order to change, I had to stop believing the negative nattering and start loosening fear's grip. Your mind won't believe you if you listen to well-meaning friends who advise you to think positively. You're not ready for that yet. You first have to slow the speed and impact of your negative thinking. Sometimes, the best thing to do is to stop looking at the problem and go for a walk, a nap, a movie—do something you enjoy, and give your mind a break from the nattering. Can you fathom the degree of fatigue our minds must suffer having to carry our negative inner critics everywhere? Find ways to escape the negative and reach for something that feels good. When you sleep, the critics also have to go to sleep! Give everyone a break, and take a rest from the incessant cacophony of judgments, comparisons, warnings, rebukes, and remonstrations.

Who wouldn't be stuck in fear with that oppressive nattering?

Exercise: Feel vs Real
Compare your Emotional Reaction to an Objective Statement.

To shift the inertia, simply start with a statement that describes the situation in which you find yourself. This should be a factual statement so as not to allow emotion to colour the phrase. Creating your statement will set off your inner-critics, which is exactly what you want. When they emerge, it's a chance to catch them out or at the very least, to actually *hear* what they're saying.

Step One "Feel"
In Step One "Feel," express the feeling in the exact words you repeat in your mind. It might be irrational, don't try to sanitise it, capture the phrase as accurately as you can.

Call to mind something you're struggling with right now. Clarify the situation. Is it about yourself, health, a relationship, work, finances, something in the family? Choose something that's close to the surface. To unlock the benefits of this exercise, make a list from each of these categories. The prominent feeling should almost be there already. Got it? Here are a few examples:

a) I'm jealous of my manager acknowledging everyone else but me!

b) I'm unworthy, that's why this relationship's doomed.

c) It's all my fault! I feel like a blundering idiot, I always drop things and now I've ruined the birthday party because I dropped the cake!

Step Two "Real"
In Step Two "Real," rephrase the feeling as an objective statement. Try to make it real. Strip away emotion to prevent it from colouring the sentence.

a) My manager acknowledges others, I could be next.

b) I've been hurt and that could be triggering the dysfunction in the relationship.

c) Mindfulness can help me deal with my clumsiness. There's more to a birthday celebration than a cake.

As you start capturing your emotional "blurts", you may find that your negative inner critics might jump in, exaggerating, and dramatising the subject:

- *My life is over.*
- *I'm such a failure.*
- *I can't believe this happened to me.*
- *I'll never work again.*
- *I'll never find love.*
- *I'm such a fuck up.*
- *What will become of me?*
- *What will people say?*
- *I'm so ashamed.*
- *I bet _____ can't wait to spread the news.*
- *_____ doesn't want me; nobody wants me.*
- *I'm not good enough.*
- *I'm over the hill.*
- *Debt is going to be the death of me.*

- *I'll never recover.*
- *How could they?*
- *I've really done it this time.*

Mind Over Natter. You have to use your mind to gain control of the nattering negative inner critics. We have an estimated 86,000 thoughts a day. They aren't really bona fide thoughts as such; they're more like mutterings, judgments, predictions, etc. We just go from day to day repeating the same stuff. When I first tried the Feel vs Real Exercise, my negative self-talk didn't stop at the first-person narrative, it launched into second person, like I was being reprimanded. Inner critics swear, don't let your pious inner princess pretend otherwise.

- *You're stupid.*
- *You're so fucking useless!*
- *You should be ashamed of yourself.*
- *What kind of loser are you?*
- *What the fuck did you think would happen?*
- *That's so typical of you.*
- *You're such a chop.*
- *You never learn.*
- *You're a big, fat, loser!*

A core component of mindfulness is learning to not identify with our negative thoughts. When we have thoughts that self-judge, our "I am" statements align with things we despise.

Has your inner critic hurt you with any of these? If you don't have a "fat" issue, then substitute the theme with an issue that's prevalent for you. Chances are your inner critics sound similar, no matter the subject.

Here's my top 10 "fat" negative nattering's

I've attacked myself with these and some are described to me by my clients.

1. *You're a big fat loser.*
2. *Hey fatty boom boom.*
3. *Look at the sight of you.*
4. *Oink Oink little piggy.*
5. *Nobody could love that.*
6. *Did you eat your twin?*
7. *Lard Ass.*
8. *Fat as houses? Try apartment blocks!*
9. *I'll never be thin.*
10. *Just give up already.*

Did anything resonate? Please take a moment to acknowledge the pain, either by hearing these insults said about you or by hearing your inner critic say them to you. Sometimes, we've inflicted these cruel comments on others in an attempt to make ourselves feel better. But it doesn't make us feel better, it only serves to diminish us. It also sets up another round of negative nattering about our hypocrisy.

So, how do you distance yourself from negative thoughts?

Don't identify with them, become mindful of the language you use. Pay attention. Notice what is going on in your mind, become aware of the judgments and labels. Have you ever questioned whether they are your judgements, or are they the judgements of others, of society? Once you have identified where they come from, and have established that they are not true, or not working for you - then choose to let them go! Choose mindfulness and compassion over criticism!

Now take a moment and review the list with compassionate awareness and see how it softens and allows you to let go of many of the statements that initially caused you pain. We can never silence the critics but we can certainly show them how to express themselves more accurately. Allow the judgements to arise, but rephrase them with compassion and mindfulness.

Remember, you are not your thoughts. You don't have to believe everything you think. *I am exhausted* can become *I notice feelings of fatigue.* Be objective about thoughts and don't let them objectify you!

Give your mind something to do rather than something to complain about. This isn't about denying what your critics see as the truth, or creating euphemisms, it's about building in some objectivity, some distance from what's observed and what's internalised as being real. I'm using "fat" as the perceived judgement but you can do this with any criticism. Change the statement into the first person. Make it personal – but don't take it personally. Don't get lost in the pain, find hope in possibility instead.

You're a big, fat loser.
Give my body the correct nutrition, rest, and exercise.

Look at the sight of you!
I'll create and live in the healthy vision I have of myself.

Nobody could love that!
I am worth loving, and once I love myself, others will too.

Fat as houses? Try apartment blocks!
Repeating what I've heard and then exaggerating it is trapping me, it's time to repeat a healthy mantra.

You'll never be thin.
I can attain and maintain optimal health.

Note:

This exercise can become emotional and painful. Most of our mindless behaviour pertains to numbing our feelings as we try to avoid experiencing them. We get stuck in addictive behaviour—alcohol, drugs, food, work, sex, etc.—as a means to distract us from feeling. Research shows that at the height of maximum emotional impact, the duration of a feeling is ninety seconds before it begins to subside. Feelings are like the light spectrum—you can't have red and deny indigo—you get the whole rainbow. There are black lines in the light spectrum in the same way there are shadows in our emotions. They all work together, and the idea of numbing feelings to cope is actually impossible, regardless of what drug (pharmaceutical or recreational) or addictive behaviour we adopt.

Expanding the "Feel" vs "Real" Exercise

How is it going with your journal? It's never too late to get one. Sometimes I draw in mine with short, broad, children's crayons. Or, enjoy the glide of colourful marker pens as they ink across a page. I might be working on a serious business proposal or a lesson plan, but the colours feel like play, and in a playful spirit, I resist less and tap into innate creativity. Brené Brown says, in *The Gifts of Imperfection*, "If we want to live a more Wholehearted life, we have to become intentional about cultivating sleep and play, and about letting go of exhaustion as a status symbol and productivity as self-worth."[1]

When you see a thought or sketch taking shape, in that playful style, you'll slow down and enjoy the connection to the work since you are literally getting in touch with your thoughts and feelings as you write. You could argue that using your phone or tablet is easier, but instead of resisting at this first bolt out the gate, I warmly encourage you to get a journal and a nice pen or pencil, and get writing and drawing. We've made inroads into clarity on thoughts and feelings, now we go even deeper towards purging and healing.

a) Start by blurting out that negative emotional statement.

b) It might sound like a child throwing a tantrum, that's okay, try and capture the tone and the words.

c) It might sound like an admonishing parent or a disgruntled sibling.

d) Be clear and as accurate as possible when you write it down. Don't filter it. Don't fight it. Don't judge yourself for feeling angry, afraid, ashamed, or silly. Simply write it down.

Examples of common blurts:

"I'm too old for this."
"I'm not good enough."
"You can't even spell. What the hell are you doing with a journal?"
"Who do you think you are?"
"I don't know how!"
"Can we do this later?"
"Worthy? You? Yeah, right! Who are you kidding?"

Exercise: Worst vs Best

1. Clearly state your "blurt", no matter what feelings it arouses.

2. Pretend to be a lawyer or a detective to build a persuasive case. Is your "blurt" a statement of fact?

    A. True

    B. False

3. Note the first few phrases that erupt from inner critics—the negative limiting beliefs. We really want to pay attention to the negative inner critics and their limiting beliefs because the solutions to our problems reside in understanding and contradicting them. Writer Julia Cameron in "The Artist's Way," calls these negative statements, "blurts." Write down the blurts. Don't clean them up. Leave them rough and raw. As you complete the list below, more of these beliefs will leak out, so dedicate a page to them, give them space, and keep writing them down. If you have more, write more.

4. Write five points (at least, more if you choose) to answer the question:
"What's the worst that could happen?"

5. Write in an answer to each of those five points:
"Which makes me think…"

6. Then, add another layer on each of the points:
"Which makes me feel …"

7. And then, add another layer:
   "Which means …"

Now that you've written down the worst, let's change the energy.

8. Write five points (at least, more if you choose) to answer the question:
   "What's the best that could happen?"

9. Write in an answer to each of those points:
   "Which makes me think …"

10. Then, add another layer on each of the points:
    "Which makes me feel …"

11. And then, add another layer:
    "Which means …"

12. Some of the "blurts" will sting, so be self-compassionate.

13. On a new page, re-write the most prominent blurts or negative limiting beliefs. Leave an empty line underneath each one.

14. Now, go back over the blurts and one by one, turn them into positive, affirming statements. Keep the statement super short, stay in the present tense, and make it personal and believable. **The best fitting affirmation, is one you create by transforming the negative critic's judgment into a positive critic's praise.**

    - from "Stupid!" to "I am learning."
    - from "I can't," to "I am willing," or "I can."
    - from "There's no hope," to "I am open to hope," or "Hopeful feels good."

The idea here is to show you that you have a choice. If you are mindful, you have the power to identify the negative nattering, and change the script. If you can think it – then you can un-think it, and change the grip it has on you. This exercise shows you just how much power you have. Use your newly realised power to change the negative nattering into positive affirming statements.

You are a composite of many emotions, neither good nor bad! These emotions either make you feel expanded or contracted. Marie Forleo in, *Everything's Figureoutable,* makes a good case for expanded or contracted, rather than positive or negative feelings. Here are her three rules of play:

Rule 1: All problems (or dreams) are figureoutable.
Rule 2: If a problem is not figureoutable, it's not really a problem—it's a fact of life or law of nature (e.g., death or gravity).
Rule 3: You may not care enough to figure this problem out or achieve this particular dream. That's okay. Find another problem or dream that ignites a blazing fire in your heart and go back to Rule 1. [2]

The connotations of positive or negative are locked in judgement, whereas thoughts and feelings that grow or constrict, offer clarity in themselves.

Use the Worst vs Best exercise with any decision or situation that arises such as the end of a relationship, a divorce, a death, the prognosis of a serious illness, emigration, changing location, etc. Your personalised affirmations will help you focus the mind. It's important to believe your affirmations. If they have come from you, they'll fit your life better than a generic motivational statement.

At this stage, you've probably had a few flare-ups, but you've met some of your inner critics and have successfully captured their limiting beliefs in the blurts they've spewed. Sometimes, they blurt out even when they know they're being investigated. Become aware (mindful) of the information they divulge. Notice you are beginning to put distance between the information and how you respond to it. You will begin to see you aren't these thoughts, and you have the power to change your thoughts. From what's the worst that could happen, to what's the best that could happen—you'll soon start to feel a psychological and emotional shift.

Your Inner Child.

Your inner child can have some serious fun here!

Your inner child allows you the opportunity to do things without restriction or censorship. The voice of the inner child echoes things you've always wanted to do. Open up and play a little with the questions—nobody said you had to be a boring adult.

Caution: around this time, if your inner child hasn't taken centre stage, your inner victim might be lurking. The victim sees everything negatively, blames everyone and everything, and takes little responsibility. If you're uncertain which voice seems to answer, ask quick and short questions. Be gentle and compassionate with yourself and your inner critics. It might surprise you to learn they aren't the enemy, they've been trying to protect you. Negative inner critics use fear and scarcity to keep you in the fold so you don't stray and risk isolation or abandonment. Once you know this, you can treat them more as compatriots and not as combatants.

If your topic pertained to work, ask some lighter questions. Phrase them in the first person, "I"

- Is it time for a career change?
- Where else could I work right now?
- What is the dream job I'd like to have?
- All logic and limits aside, what did I want to do when I was a kid?

When you begin to push back against the negative natterings you'll begin to ignite feelings of *hope*! You're no longer wallowing in what you don't want, but basking in the possibilities of a new way of being.

Notice how your feelings have changed. Previously, you were full of doubt and focused on pain and shame and hopelessness. Now, the negative momentum has slowed sufficiently for you to extricate yourself from the grip of fear, and you can explore possibilities and even entertain your life's dreams. Get even more relaxed about the questions. Let's imagine your topic involved your intimate relationship.

- Who said relationships had to be hard?
- If there were no limits or judgments, how might this relationship evolve?
- What've I always dreamed of doing in this partnership but never got the chance to do?

- What delights me?

The inner child usually likes to finish the line of questioning. Let's say your initial topic was about finances …

- *Hey, I know—let's buy a lotto ticket!*
- *How about dog walking?*
- *Imagine being the voice of an animated movie character.*
- *What about Zorro? Can we be Zorro?* (The inner child can also take over, so manage the situation kindly).

I hope this exercise showed you how you can make an ally out of the mind that was tormenting you. Sometimes an uninterrogated thought makes us feel worse. Don't confront thoughts, clarify them. The Worst vs Best exercise brings thoughts into focus.

"My life's a mess, what can I do about it?" To answer the question, let's first address the labelling and judgment. Life is challenging, and there are ups and downs for everyone. Be more mindful, and judge yourself less. Try not to label—most are hurtful and a mindless way to treat yourself. We're in forward motion—life is unfolding one breath at a time. The idea here is to embrace the unfolding and not sit in the idea that your life's a mess.

Compassion is a beautiful, expansive feeling. We don't feel like we're missing out or losing out or running out when we offer compassion to ourselves and others. When we're compassionate, it's often reciprocated. Becoming aware of your blurts and turning them into positive statements to use as daily affirmations, is a giant stride towards clarity. Your interaction with your inner critics is the start of awareness. Mindfulness will help you process what the inner critics believe, and the frequency and veracity with which they say it. Beliefs aren't necessarily true; they're merely repeated ideas.

This exercise can be exhausting, so rest a moment. Do something kind for your critics, for your mind, for your body, and for your soul. Be extra gentle now, and offer yourself the soothing compassion that acknowledges you've done some significant healing work. You are trying to overcome the pain of your negative inner critics so you can transform your life from calamity to clarity. May you enjoy everyday mindfulness and be blessed with health, wealth, love, and happiness.

Be Bright, Be Brief and Be Mindful

- Breathing is a portal to mindfulness.
- Multi-tasking is mindlessness. It causes exhaustion and muddles the mind.
- Focus on one thing at a time.
- Whether we created the pain or not, we can stop perpetuating it.
- Mindlessness crumbles in the face of planning.
- Plan the night before, and stay mindful during the day.
- Don't get so blinkered that you can't see into your imagination—keep an open mind.
- Don't allow your inner critic to narrate your story for you. Take control.
- Play. Have fun, and enjoy.
- Feel vs Real: convert childlike tantrums into objective statements.
- Notice the range of voices gaining clarity: inner critic, inner child, inner victim.
- Start planning and designing rather than reacting and clamouring.
- Fear paralyses—create a statement of fact from a childlike blurt to describe your actual situation.
- Ask questions in an objective, playful way to help you understand the situation.
- Give yourself permission to play.

- Start your questions logically, and then allow your inner child to have fun with the possibilities.
- What's the worst vs What's the best that could happen?

Chapter Three Meditation
Mindlessness—My Life's a Mess, What Can I Do about It?

Welcome, and thank you for coming into this mindfulness practice created especially for *Mind Over Natter*. We meditate on the idea that your current experience of life is making you unhappy, and you want to make changes. You've been tolerating this problem, discomfort, depression, sadness, etc., for a long time. Let's call it mindlessness. You've come to realise that you just don't want to feel this way anymore. You are ready for something different.

We set our intention at the start of this meditation:

- We recognise that we don't want to feel mindless.
- We're willing to engage in mindfulness.

Let's take a moment to settle into this experience now. Sit with your back upright, be relaxed but alert. Invite your body to get comfortable. Find the balance within your posture so you can sustain that position for a few minutes. Take a deep breath in to mark your transition from where you were to where you are now.

Breathe in and breathe out, release. We draw our awareness inside, leaving all the external noise behind—the noise of the room, the noise of our thoughts, and the noise of our feelings. Breathe in through the nose, then breathe out through the nose. Ensure you're not stiffening your shoulders when you breathe in. Now, breathe out. Release. Relax. Ease away from the mind and drop down into the heart centre. Become aware of your heart. Feel compassion as you entrust yourself to this meditation.

Starting with the top of your head, bring your awareness to your scalp and sense relaxing energy moving down over your face. Soften around your eyes and forehead. As you breathe, relax around the nose. Loosen your cheekbones. Relax your jaw, mouth and chin. Let the tongue relax behind the lips. Release tension in your throat and at the neck. Relax. Sense relaxation across your shoulders. Relax the chest. Letting go. Letting go. Notice your upper back. Release the tightness through your middle back and down to your lower back. Allow your abdomen to relax now. Sense all your internal organs and give them permission to relax inside you. Just gently let go. Feel the relaxation expand through your upper arms, to your elbows, and your forearms. Feel your wrists. Relax your right hand and then your left hand. Let your thumbs and fingers release and let go of any tension. Feel the presence of your body as a whole. Take your awareness to your skin, the largest organ of the body. Release the tension of your skin. Observe the contact points on the cushion, the floor, or the chair. Sink deeper. Relax. Have a sense of relaxation through your pelvis. You are experiencing your body not thinking about your body.

Slacken the muscles in your buttocks. Relax the muscles and the joints of your upper legs. Relax the front of the legs. Now relax the back of the legs. Notice your knees. Letting go of any aches. Draw your awareness down the shins and then round to the back of your calves. Relax through the ankles. Become aware of your heels. Sense your feet as they rest on the floor. Feel the soles of your feet. Then the upper feet. Notice your toes, relax and let go.

Take a deep breath and on the out breath relax. Imagine a wave of even deeper relaxation washing over your whole body from your head all the way down to your toes and into the ground. Travel with the relaxation. Notice it move across your skin, into all the joints, through the muscles, the ligaments, tendons, internal organs. Relaxation drops down, down, down, the whole body and leaves through the feet. Relax. Let go. Release. Breathe.

When we're caught in mindlessness, we've no sense of our body. We're stuck in our minds, and we believe every thought that comes up. When you focus on your body, you are less distracted by your thoughts.

If you noticed pain anywhere in your body, send healing energy to that location. Imagine that part of your body warming up and releasing the pain.

As we breathe in, we notice that thoughts drift into our awareness. Just as easily as we breathe out, thoughts drift out of our awareness.

Pay attention to parts of your body that are neutral or that feel good. Send your focus to these places. Enjoy feeling good.

Continue to meditate. Become aware of the quality of presence in your body. As thoughts come up, let them dissolve away. Slowly, usher your awareness back to your breath. Breathe in. With mindfulness, I am breathing in. Breathe out. With mindfulness, I am breathing out.

Feel the calm in your body in this present moment. Kindness. Acceptance. Compassion. Healing. Breathe in. Breathe out.

Before we leave this deep relaxation, we remind ourselves of our intention. We recognise that we don't want to be mindless, that we can intend to live with mindfulness.

Take this relaxed, peaceful feeling with you into everything you do today. Rest gently tonight, with kindness for yourself and for your body. Bring to mind the faces of those nearest to you. Recognise your love for them, and experience gratitude for their life and for your own. May you be mindful, and may those around you enjoy being mindful.

When you are ready, and in your own time, open your eyes. Take a deep breath in and release this meditation, returning fully to the room.

We fill our heart space with gratitude. Thank you.

May you be healthy, wealthy, loved, and happy.

CHAPTER FOUR
LOOK WHO'S TALKING
(AND WHO'S LISTENING)

"Speak in such a way that others love to listen to you. Listen in such a way that others love to speak to you."

Anonymous

Too LOUD!

Too LOUD!
Mind cacophony, peace-thieving noise.
Sense separation;
Turn it down so I can see, so I can taste, so I can feel.
Distraction, confusion, incessance—even in sleep.
Memories, worries, strategies;
People, places, problems.
Stuck mind, repeating mind, conflicted, inflicting mind.
What's the sound of silence to ears that have forgotten?
How am I hearing inaudible thoughts?
The tyranny of their seeming silence,
When really, they are screaming!
Or is that me? Where am I in all of this?
Relentless judgement, perpetual commentary.
Where is the kindness of reprieve?
I'm deaf to the yearning of the voice that hoped once.
What?
I can't hear!
I long to listen.

What's That, You Say?

Our inner monologue impacts our sense of self and how we think about the world. It can help us create a beautiful environment right in the midst of a torturous situation. But for the most part, we don't use this power for good. Instead, we allow ourselves to run on autopilot in perpetual commentary and judgement, which pushes us into negativity, painful states of mind, and troubling emotions which create tension in the body, messed up behaviour, and ultimately, to illness.

In the 1989 movie, *Look Who's Talking,* Kirstie Allie's character is a single, career-minded woman, left on her own to have the baby of a married man. An unexpected romance develops with a cab driver, played by John Travolta, but he's not the leading man of the movie. The highlight of the film is the point-of-view of the new-born baby boy, narrated by Bruce Willis.

What's fun about the film is giving an adult voice to a baby. What's fun about life is giving attention to the voices that narrate and speak to us throughout our lifetime. If someone is doing the talking, someone has to be listening. Michael A. Singer goes into some amazing internal dialogues in his book, "The Untethered Soul: The Journey Beyond Yourself." I wholeheartedly recommend it since, as he says, "There is nothing more important to true growth than realizing that you are not the voice of the mind - you are the one who hears it." [1]

It might seem obvious, but many of us are stuck in mental turmoil, unaware that *we* are the ones listening to the nattering of our inner critics. Without mindfulness, we get stuck listening and believing everything our inner voices say. As you progress deeper into your practice, you will develop heightened powers of discernment, and greater compassion for yourself and even for the voices. You will also become astute at realizing you can change the voices—or at least modify their messages, calm their cruelty, and direct them towards your dreams.

The Story of Our Lives as Narrated to Us by Our Minds

Are you familiar with the saying, "Seeing is believing?" We see something and believe it to be true. If we repeatedly hear something, we believe that to be true, too, because voices carry. When we live on auto-pilot, as so many of us do, we aren't even aware of the persistence of our inner criticisms. If we do become conscious of the painful admonishments, we might interpret them as stress, and then incessant noise becomes a cycle of anxiety. Thankfully, once a voice has your attention, you might discover that it calms down. By listening to the comments and discerning their validity, we can lower the volume of the voices, and then, either follow or reject their advice. Your inner voice is formed by internalizing and repeating other people's viewpoints, which in turn influences your opinion of yourself. Your body is also trying to speak to you. If you get caught up in perfection and drive yourself too hard, finding fault with everything you do, your body might have to show up sick, just so you can slow down and rest.

Meet the Inner Critic Clan

Not all voices are negative. As I've suggested, there are both positive and negative voices in my head. Similar voices are likely to be in yours too (to a greater or lesser extent). We all have them. I differentiate them into "The Inner Critic Clans," headed by the Chieftain, "Judge Mental."

In Ireland, the Gaelic term for family or *of the family*, is clan. I created an anthropomorphised version of my family of inner critics. The negative clan is Clan Calamity and the cheerier lot are Clan Clarity. They also like to be referred to as the Calamity Clan or the Clarity Clan (which seems like the same thing, though they assure me it isn't.) Actually, it's a little more complicated than semantics and differentiating one side as negative and the other as positive.

Taskmaster Tara Malloy ("Tara" means crag or tower, and "Malloy" in Irish means noble chief) can get up in my grill about getting stuff done, but she's often right. Thanks to her insistence, I feel an immense relief when I complete a task.

The more you develop your mindfulness practice, the more you will be able to differentiate between your inner voices. You may even name clans of your own. Perhaps yours is simply one positive voice and one negative voice. I'm a fan of embellishing, so it was a fun way of using my awareness to identify and then relate to them. It allowed me to put some distance between what I heard in my mind and what I'd think, say, or do about it.

Sometimes, we're fortunate enough to be mindfully present in any given moment, but holding that present moment awareness takes practice. Good anchoring techniques include: breath awareness, paying attention to the environment, really noticing body sensations, and releasing attachments to thoughts and emotions. My friends often tease me after a mindless spell where I've knocked something, spilled something, or tripped over something. They say, "Ditsy Dame! I see Calamity's in town."

My Inner Critic Clan

Chieftain Judge Mental
with Clarity and Calamity

Inner Critics, from Left to Right: Clarity,
Judge Mental, Calamity

Clan Composite, From Left to Right: DJ, Fionnuala Tremulous (Fear), Clare Breathe-easy (Calm), Boohoo Bad Shoes (Blame), Ragnar Ragemeister (Rage), Venge (Vengeful), Snoot (Superiority Complex), Happy Joe Lucky, Penelope Perfect (Perfectionist).

Look Who's Talking (and Who's Listening)

Calamity Clan Member	Characteristic
Calamity Knockherblock	Calamity
Cash-strapped Stevens	Poverty Consciousness
Aggie Worrywart	Anxiety
Deborah Devastate	Depression
Sab O'Tage	Saboteur
Darah McDark	Doom
Penelope Perfect	Perfectionist
Pro Pro	Procrastination
Tara Malloy	Taskmaster (Coach, when she's in a good mood)
Terry O'Flatley	Fatigue
Sir Forgetalot	Forgetful
Fionnuala Tremulous	Fear
Podge	Comfort Eater
Ragnar Ragemeister	Rage
Innes of the Please Love Me People	Insecurity
Jayda Green-Envy	Jealousy
Feelbad McCracken III	Guilt
Cranky Stuckspanner	Killjoy
Doubt Monger	Doubt
Reeva No-Go	Resistance
Boohoo Bad Shoes	Blame
Snoot	Superiority Complex
Venge	Vengeance
	Inner Parent
	Inner Adult
	The Body

Clarity Clan Member	Characteristic
Clarity Clearview	Clarity
Sophie Kindheart	Sympathy
Kelly Kindheart (Sophie's sister)	Kindness
Clare Breathe-Easy	Calm
Harry O'Smile	Happiness
Olivia Untwist	Organiser
Makenzie Make-It-Happen	Motivation
Professoré	Teacher
Keegan	My Dalmatian as a Spirit Guide
Emphatica	Decisiveness
Cuán (little wolf)	Courage
Kid Kane	Inner Child
Rezzy Keepherlit	Resilience
Jennifer Generous	Generosity
Happy Joe Lucky	Easy-going
Briana (noble, virtuous)	Belief (warrior who takes AIM)
Vickytickytoria	Success
	Love
	Intuition
	Soul
	Inner Parent
	Inner Adult
	The Body

Introducing the Inner Critics, the Voices in Our Heads

You'll notice the Inner Adult; Inner Parent and The Body can present as either calamity or clarity inner critics. Here's an example of how the critics sound.

The inner critic:
"One inner voice is bad enough, but now she's saying there are multiple voices?"

The inner child:
"This is fun. Wonder how many voices there are? What if they get into a fight?"

The inner adult:
"Watch what you say."

The inner parent:
"Don't upset yourself with this voice or that. Listen to the still, small voice."

The soul:
(Silence at first). Then, a feeling of deep, kind, beautiful, and peaceful love.

There are a few more layers beneath these cursory voices. Have you ever mindlessly drifted off in thought when someone was talking to you, and you haven't heard a word they've said? You *were* listening, but not to them. You were listening to your inner voice, instead.

Your inner critic might not want you to discover it; it might guard its anonymity so you don't expose it. It wants to carry on talking so you can listen. It likes to be in control and uses the voice of another influential person in your life to avert detection. Here's what I mean: Have you ever said something to your child and realized you sounded just like your mother or father? When you were a child, you made promises to yourself that you'd never do that to your children. Yet, here you are being a mini-me parent, echoing: "Money doesn't grow on trees!"

One thing we can't afford to do is to pretend we don't have an inner critic. Our inner critic is part of the creative team that helps plant ideas in our minds. Decades in the broadcasting industry have taught me that criticism is necessary, and it's not all negative. So, whilst they're called the inner *critics*, there are some *supporting* voices in there too. Also, we don't learn in a vacuum- repeating the same things. Sometimes, we need someone to critique us so we can learn and change.

Ideas can fade to nothing, but many are painfully birthed into the material world, resulting in a discontented life. Wouldn't you rather know what's being said about you than live in a false sense of comfort? I encourage you not to be complacent. Look who's talking and more importantly, remember that *you* are listening. A part of you (consciously or unconsciously) is affected by the comments of your inner critic. Have you ever blamed someone for bringing you down, making you miserable, or hurting your feelings? And have you ever considered you were doing all those things to yourself? It's dangerously easy to slide into complacency and before you know it, you're complying with things you truly don't like. Mediocrity isn't good enough for you. Choose more wisely, expect more from yourself, become invested in the tone and content of your inner dialogue, and change it if it doesn't serve you or those you love. As the "Too LOUD!" poem says, when the mind is conflicted, it then inflicts harm on itself and others.

When you tune in to the mental nattering, you will notice that you are neither the voices nor the thoughts in your head. Not all thoughts are audible—some wash up as feelings, some seem defused in a faint memory, and others are barely detectable because they're more like sensations. Not being attuned to sensations makes us unavailable to their inherent wisdom. Have you ever had a sick feeling in your gut only moments before something went wrong? That was voiceless intuition speaking without words. Each of us has the ability to tap into the invisible force of our intuition or our sixth sense. Sometimes, the inner message is subtle, almost imperceptible. Other times, it's a strong aversion, even breaking out in a skin rash or becoming physically ill. It's not only our inner critics who talk to us; our bodies also communicate. The body tells the truth, ask any body language expert. For our ancestors, survival depended on being aware of the tribe's communication strategy and staying connected as part of the group rather than apart from it. Finely tuned intuition and instinct meant you got to live another day.

Our need for inclusion sometimes manifests itself in modern times as "approval addiction". But the roots of the need for approval lie in an archetypal environment that was either hostile or helpful. Whether we actively seek the approval of others or not, there's an imperative need that runs deeper than logic (perhaps even beneath our consciousness) for acceptance, interaction, and involvement. The impetus for fight, flight, or freeze initiates a small part of our brain called the amygdala. It is unable to distinguish a life and death situation from surviving an altercation with your wife, a reprimand from your boss, or the panic that only a glare from a teenager can beset.

Actual danger or the perceived threat of danger aren't differentiated in the brain, so the impact on the body is an adrenalized state based on our thoughts. That idea, speech, project, spreadsheet, laundry, diet, gym contract, new relationship, important discussion with your child, job, etc. causes stress, which is leaking into your body. When left unattended, it will make you sick and could ultimately cost you your life. I'm not being overdramatic—it's a scientific fact that stress kills.

Our thinking is part of our problem, and our inner critics will sabotage the very things we want if we continue to ignore them! Sometimes, merely contemplating the need to push past difficult thoughts was reason enough for me to stop trying. Even the smallest decisions seemed too much. I planned to go out for a meal with friends, but I'd cancel at the last minute. If I forced myself to go, I couldn't decide what to order. Once the meals were served, I became "plate-envious" since someone else's choice always seemed preferable to mine. I was too damn tired. In bouts of depression, I had neither apathy nor ambivalence—I had nothing. I wasn't fully numb because I could sense pain, but I felt empty. I felt like I couldn't access inspiration. I didn't care if change would lead to restoration because I fundamentally didn't care about myself. I didn't think of it as laziness, lack of resolve, or self-sabotaging. I justified not trying as hard-earned sensibility. Where the heck has sensibility got me? When I review my life, I see sensibility may have worked occasionally, but mainly it didn't really advance my prospects. What I've come to appreciate is there's a wonder-world of possibility on the other side of a negative inner critic's belief.

A world of possibility is waiting, bursting for you to use mind over natter to overcome your negative critics and make that all-important first move—getting ready to get ready. It's preparation before action, and the positive inner critics from the Clarity Clan will rally to your rescue, encouraging:

> *You can do it.*
> *Go on!*
> *That's it. You've got this!*
> *You thought _____was impossible and yet, you did it.*
> *Things often seem tough at the start.*
> *Give it a whirl!*
> *Forget about the worst, what's the best that could happen?*
> *Surprise yourself.*
> *Make a start, see how it goes.*
> *Lighten up a little. What if it's fun?*
> *I say, 'Yes!*
> *Okay, I'll give it a go.*
> *Sure, why not?*
> *Try it, see if you like it.*
> *What if this is your purpose?*
> *You're magnificent. (Crickets SFX from the Calamity Clan).*

Look Who's Talking (and Who's Listening)

Caution: Your Calamity Clan will give the Clarity Clan only so much mental space before they slither in with niggling doubt sidewinders. Sometimes, they come at you, guns blazing, shooting you down before you can build positive momentum. Sometimes they chuck a spanner in the works. Sometimes, they drip doubt into your dreams. That's why mind over natter is important; stay on task, stay mindful, and be clear of your intention behind the changes you want to make! Here's what's interesting, the inner critics do a lot of talking but they also have to listen when you take control. The positive critics love being set tasks and you can recruit them to help you.

Get excited—it's really important to feel good about change.

Exercise: Name Your Clans

1. Name your own clans (1 = positive & 1 = negative).

2. Then name the members of each clan. I find this really helpful as it puts distance between me and my inner critics. For example: If I'm too closely identified with a fearful thought, it helps to observe, *Oh look, Fionnuala Tremulous* (who represents fear) *is frightened about doing a Facebook Live session.* I shift the impact of the fearful thought and slow the momentum of more frightening thoughts. Introduce this playful tool, consider thoughts as expressions of clan members. *Wouldn't you know it, old Fi's brought Doubt Monger – those two go everywhere together!*

3. If you need some more inspiration beyond the clans I've suggested, search for a list of emotional states. Consider

dimensions of pleasant-unpleasant, tension-relaxation. Also, think about opposites and how they impact each other.

4. Do this exercise in a spirit of playfulness. Don't be surprised if your version of Reeva No-go (resistance) surfaces. They say naming gives us power. Name your resistance and soon you will see a shift beyond mental patterns and habitual behaviour that block you.

5. Sketch your critics, draw speech bubbles or find images that represent them.

Tuning into the Clans for clarity

Imagine the clans are DJ's on your personal radio station. Broadcasting requires a transmitter (broadcaster) and a receiver. When a radio is being tuned there is white noise or static between the stations. Then there is sudden clarity and potency from one small point on the receiver. Tuning in to your inner critics is just like tuning into a specific radio station. Remember you broadcast and receive your own thoughts. When we become aware of our thoughts, we can identify which station we've selected. Have you ever tuned in to the station of anxiety, confusion and not good enough? The DJ's on that particular station are your inner critics and they are relentless. Those shows are a misery, so why do we endure them? Close attention to the content of our broadcasts makes an enormous difference in our lives.

Remember that radio wave vibrations are like the energetic feelings or vibrations of our thoughts: invisible to the human eye. Thoughts, like radio waves, are moving all around and through us, affecting our moods. Have you ever walked in on a discussion and felt a bad vibe? Like you were unwanted there, or not meant to hear the conversation? You are constantly walking in on your own mental nattering's. It's no fun listening to anxiety and it's no fun broadcasting anxiety. It's a delight tuning in to joy and it's wonderful transmitting joy. Be mindful of what you broadcast and receive. Ever been at an event and the speaker takes the microphone to speak but instead you hear that awful, loud feedback? That painful, electronic noise makes you want to cover your ears to protect them. Feedback in terms of your personal radio station, means you don't get to cover your ears, you are talking and you are listening all the time. It's your choice: good vibes or painful noises.

The body and mind share a feedback mechanism too, each one influences the other. Our body and mind pair to create a circuit of thoughts, beliefs, feelings and actions. Even if you are not conscious of your thoughts, you will experience them sooner or later in your body. Thoughts vary in tone and volume, some are like perpetual nagging, others lash loudly. Lately I've been deliberately tuning in to the optimistic, encouraging broadcasts full of love and enthusiasm! Negative thoughts have more resistance and slow momentum and positive thoughts flow with ease and speed up momentum. What do you want to broadcast and receive; wellness or illness? You broadcast energy and when you tap into momentum you can speed up that energy to get either,

1. good results faster

or

2. worse results faster.

Here's a poem I just wrote about momentum.

Momentum

"Slow down, calm down, pipe down - you can't get there from here!" they say.
WHO are the "*they*" in "they say"?
Whom are they to say?
Forget about them, I'm irreverently dream-abuzz hopeful,
I'm sparkling and effervescent,
I'm glitter-scattered,
I'm hurtling forward!
Then I remember and gravity, gravely grinds,
Alerting doubt and guilt who twin with plagues,
That crash me off the bridge, plummeting downward.
Deep dark, dreary-dump-down-doomed.
Downward and inward into the abyss.
Despite the drag and the drudge,
My dreams flicker their last hope.
Slow down, calm down, pipe down - you can't get there from here.
Word-catching, thought-busting,
The flame ignites
Stoke the fire!
Clickety-click, clickety-click, back on track
Clickety-click, clickety-clack
Keep her lit!
For this is how I get there from here!

The "Momentum" poem describes a range of emotions. Even positive or expansive emotions transition. The nature of change is that transience applies to negative emotions and difficult situations too. There is always movement. Even if you're feeling disheartened right now, somewhere inside you, there is that last flicker of hope. There is something you've always dreamed of doing, being, having. The poem ends with a decision to act. Failure to act, kept me in victim mode for decades. I knew I had to change, but I allowed fear to stop me. This created a whole range of additional problems. I encourage you to make that change. Act right now, where you are, with what you have. Even if that action is just taking a breath and scanning your heart for what you love. Change will happen anyway. Do you want the change to go from bad to worse or would you like to slow that momentum and get back on track towards your hopes and dreams?

*Life applauds action,
but the root
of all wellbeing
is alignment.*

#mindovernatterbook

My life began to change when I stopped asking, "Why me?" and started questioning alignment.

What is alignment?
How do I know when I'm in alignment?
And what am I supposed to align with?
How do I get back into alignment if I lose it?

Alignment is about arrangement and correct relative positions. In other words, alignment means that parts of something are in the proper position relative to each other. Of what, you might ask? Of your life and your relationship to it. Are you living your dream life, feeling harmonious and in tune with your purpose? Or are you trapped in a nightmare? What was your day like today? If you were out of alignment, perhaps you experienced feelings of anxiety, craving, judging etc. If you were aligned, you may have resonated with a quality of wholeheartedness where you felt authentic and present. We're born with an internal alignment gauge. This instrument measures our distance from where we are to where we want to be in units of feelings. The better you feel, the more aligned you are.

So, what is the alignment gauge? It's our feelings, augmented by intuition (or gut instinct). A good way to tune into intuition is to drop into awareness through mindfulness. Although our conscience is partly produced through conditioning, our sense of right and wrong can also offer guidance. With mindfulness, however, we're focusing on awareness rather than judgement. How do you know if you are in or out of alignment? How do you feel? Look who's talking. If the inner critics are nattering at you, they know you are out of alignment. Your body knows the truth, even if you try to deny it. Only you can answer the question of what to align with. Draw your awareness inwards rather than trying to find alignment, externally. It's an internal state that feels effortless. Alignment evokes our deepest aspirations, so tune into what you want. We get stuck and forget about what we want in our lives. I'm not talking about flashy cars and mansions, it's deeper than that—alignment touches purity, love, freedom, it's a sense of awakening to your soul's purpose. That feeling of discomfort, dissatisfaction or even disease, is an indication that you are out of alignment with your heart's desire.

>Alignment = feel good.
>Out of alignment = feel bad.

Through mindfulness you can get more in touch with how you are feeling and then adjust your alignment.

Perhaps Mindfulness Is Misnamed

What we continue to learn from science, something spirituality has been guiding us to believe for eons, is consciousness isn't limited to the brain. There's nothing at all to suggest consciousness rests exclusively in the brain or even in the mind, since each cell in the body acts with consciousness in order to perform its daily, complicated, intermolecular functions. The mind is so ethereal, we struggle to describe it, locate it, or even fully comprehend it. This is why mindfulness is perhaps misnamed, since, by virtue of its title, we assume mindfulness refers to only the mind. We mistakenly infer the mind to be the brain. Yet, mindfulness pertains to all aspects of being: awareness, thoughts, senses, feelings, emotions, the physical body, the natural world, the planet, the universe, and the entire cosmos.

If we live with a closed mindset and a closed-off heart, we can't even conceive new possibilities. I like the meme that says: "we're better giving people a bit of our heart rather than a piece of our mind". In Eastern languages, the word for mind includes heart. Isn't it more enticing to be open to exploration, staying open, and being compassionate rather than shutting out possibilities by maintaining a rigid mind? We aren't just blobs of flesh and water living out a sentence until we die. We're participating in a miracle. Creation is a marvel, and not only are we priceless components, we get to be creators in our right. How many of us are *alive* in our lives?

Credit Peanuts with Charlie Brown and Snoopy by Charles Monroe Schulz.

I'm with Snoopy on this subject - and until that moment of physical death—I'd like to be *alive* in my life! Our physical bodies integrate a multitude of systems. By understanding how they function, we can understand what's happening inside our bodies and how what's happening inside our minds influences everything. What's incredible is how these systems interact seamlessly with each other without our conscious intervention. If we try unpack the systems to view them in isolation, it diminishes the essence of how they function. They work with each other and through each other in an interconnectedness that can be enhanced or diminished based on our thoughts. Part of my struggle with my sense of happiness is rooted in my sense of separation. Accepting there's no separation, as "A Course in Miracles" repeatedly emphasizes, has been a source of restoration for me. Moving away from a separated ego self, to a connected sense of belonging, is a powerful way to appreciate the part we play in life. To feel embraced and welcomed enables us to share in the reciprocity of life as we shift our identity from separated to included, accepted, and connected. If we understand our whole being is listening to our thoughts, we become more mindful about monitoring them, and increasingly more motivated to change them—more placebo, less nocebo.

The Marvels of The Body Mind

I was talking about the Limbic System (motivation, emotion, learning, and memory) to my sister, Lisa, who made a joke about an internal limbo party, singing, "How low can you go?" The irony is she was right on the money—the Limbic System does determine how low we go emotionally. Limbic thinking is often associated with fear. When the Limbic System takes over, we're in "developmental arrest". Even when there is no immediate threat, our body retains the physiological impulse to deal with something that *might* go wrong. Being personally familiar with the constricting feelings of fear, and often being stuck in a fear trance, I was eager to learn more. In "Radical Acceptance," Dr Tara Brach explains the significance of coming to terms with fear.

> Letting go into fear, accepting it, may seem counterintuitive. Yet because fear is an intrinsic part of being alive, resisting it means resisting life. The habit of avoidance seeps into every aspect of our life: It prevents us from loving well, from cherishing beauty with and around us, from being present to the moment. [2]

Since starting this book—and it's taken a while to write—I've observed a distinct change in my life. My sister and I are both calmer, more compassionate, and generally lighter about the challenges we face. We're lighter in our bodies, too. Yes, mindfulness can help you lose weight! I prefer to say, *gain health*, lest the weight should ever find see it's no longer lost and comes galumphing back to me!

You will discover your life is eminently more manageable when you are no longer held hostage by what your negative inner critics dictate. By playing a little more and not taking the whole internal dialogue thing too seriously, you'll find it easier to handle stressful situations. Your resilience will improve, and your self-confidence will sky-rocket.

Limbo(ic) Dancing

The Limbic System got me thinking about limbo dancing! The object of the dance is to bend backwards to move forward under a pole without knocking it down, right? We do this in life sometimes, don't we? We bring ourselves down with our negative nattering and then bend over backwards, all the while trying, to move forward into living an authentic and mindful life.

This is the work so many of us are engaged in—trying to uncover and discover what drives us, what causes our attachments and why these evoke our behaviour. We don't live in separation or isolation, so everything we think, say, feel, and do, impacts us as individuals and impacts those around us. Becoming mindful is not merely for our restoration and sense of wellbeing, but it also benefits others and the planet in general. We all count. We all matter. Even when we do nothing, there's a ripple effect. What kind of influence would you like to be? Imagine what your aligned action could create?

Emotions

To achieve mind over natter, it's imperative to understand what's happening in the mind, how this contributes to the emotions we feel, the sensations we experience in our bodies, the actions we take, and the life we experience. In terms of the brain, where do our emotions reside? Science would say they reside in the Limbic System, the set of structures in the brain that deal with emotions and memory. This is where our involuntary or unconscious and endocrine (hormone) functions are regulated. This is the place where necessary functions happen and over which we think we don't have control - but perhaps we do have at least a degree of influence. What's interesting is the Limbic System responds to emotional stimuli, and it, to some degree, reinforces our behaviour. If we understand how the Limbic System functions, is it possible for us to reverse engineer the sequence? Instead of being a victim to what our inner critics say, perhaps we can harness their power to echo what we'd prefer to say. Research suggests that the gut has even more of a role to play than our brain in terms of our intelligence and the secretion of hormones. Trust your gut instincts.

Prevention is always better than cure. If we know we have the potential to react or overreact to a stimulus, doesn't it make sense to equip ourselves with the tools to handle the situation? So instead of always unconsciously reacting, we can learn to consciously respond!

Think about that for a minute.

Do I always unconsciously react to the natter in my head, or do I take a minute to listen to the natter, decide if it's true or not, then possibly re-frame it, take a breath, and only then respond? That's what being mindful is all about, taking a minute to assess the natter and consciously *respond* to it! Is it possible to expand the time frame between the stimulus and our response? Can we manage the severity of our response? Is it even possible to get ahead of the situation so we avoid having to respond at all? The answer is YES to all these questions.

It's important to look at who's talking because if the inner voices are merely reacting and causing us to be reactive, then we're stuck harvesting the same old crap. If you were to eat your words, would they be palatable or poisonous? Mindfulness counteracts automatic behaviour, producing delicious, nutritious thoughts, feelings and actions. Organically avoid volatile outcomes before they happen. Mindfulness tills the mind for expansive growth. Rather than trying to fix each sick or dying leaf, listen to the kinder, warmer thoughts that stem from the root, blossoming into that scrumptious banquet of delights I mentioned at the start.

Thinking about Thoughts

I don't know about you, but it's a bit of a brain-bender for me to think about my thoughts. To contemplate a concept that asked me to use the very mechanism which was causing my pain seemed too cerebral for me. I found I couldn't hold on to the thinking process itself since new thoughts kept interrupting my enquiry. To try and interrogate the process to make it easier for me, I tried writing down the thoughts one at a time. Philosophers have long been fascinated with the question of thought and language. Mostly, thoughts are shaped in the mind and then formulated through language. That's why we're so different—our language informs our thoughts. If we want to understand each other, it's more than culture and location. It's about the fundamentals inherent in language. In the silence of the soul, a sense of deep understanding and acceptance supersedes language since it connects more profoundly than words. It's the hardest thing in the world to get to soul silence, but we can sense fleeting moments of soul silence in meditation.

It's difficult to think about a thought and not have language try to shape and describe it. I've learnt that as soon as I give impetus to the struggle, I inadvertently leave the door open for judgment. My thought becomes a voice. Sometimes I imagine my critics gathered together, waiting for me to wake up so I can give them back their voices which often fly at me in a frenzy of interjections:

I need to pee.
Oh, thank goodness you're awake.
About fucking time!
No time for all that affirmation and Morning Pages bullshit. Get up.
Why do you even bother? That's pie in the sky stuff!
Pie in the sky. Pie in the sky. Hate it when people say that.
"Shut up, you!"
I'm so tired.
Wonder if I need to get something for it?

Exercise more, then you'll sleep better.
Drama queen.
Right, pages first, then see if Lisa wants to come with me to take Rhiley for a walk.
That's it, go ahead and grab your smartphone.
No man, I'm really tired. Okay I'll just check messages quick.

This all happens almost simultaneously, and I bet that it took longer for you to read those thoughts than it took for my inner critics to conjure them up and fire them at me. Thoughts flow at lightning speed, bringing feelings and body sensations which can strike you down if you're not mindful. "Kill them with kindness,"—since I was a kid, I've had a tiny conflict about that saying. It seems so un-spiritual.

Exercise: Cultivating Kindness

Take a moment to think about kindness. In your journal, write the answers to these questions.

Draw pictures or cut out images from magazines that reflect your interpretation of kindness.

1. Can you visualise an image that depicts kindness?
2. What does kindness feel like?
3. Have you experienced kindness?
4. Where do you feel kindness in your body, in your chest, say, around your heart?
5. Is there anyone, anything, or any place that evokes feelings of kindness in you?

6. Have you been kind to a person, a pet, a place?

7. When we have affection for something or someone, kindness seems easier to access. Imagine what it feels like to be kind to someone who has your affection.

8. Can you feel the difference between kindness and affection and yet how both feel good? How are you feeling right now?

9. How do you feel about offering kindness to someone or something you don't like?

10. Are you kind to yourself?

11. Can you forgive yourself for not being kind in the past?

12. Describe your life if you could cultivate more kindness.

Could you access kindness? Could you feel what it is like to receive kindness and how it feels to give kindness? Whether you are giving or receiving kindness, it feels warm and loving. As you did this exercise, were you aware of any changes (however slight) in your mind, your mood, or your body? Did you sense a softening of your facial expression? Perhaps the pain in your body felt lighter?

Look at who's talking and who's listening—it's *you*—but which version of you? Be kind! Stop tolerating what you don't want, and do more of what you do want. Don't be a victim to those inner critics who want to take you down. Tune in to feel good broadcasts.

The Thinking Mind, the Feeling Body

Minds think, that's what they do—it's how they operate. Body's feel largely in response to thoughts. This is neither good nor bad; it's simply the nature of the mind body connection. They can also influence each other in reverse. So, a pleasant physical experience can contribute to a pleasant mental experience.

*We habitually
rehash the past
and rehearse the future,
which effectively thieves away
the present.*

#mindovernatterbook

If our thoughts are hectic, chances are the stress levels in our body will mirror that chaos. Being present in moment-to-moment awareness, slowing down the judgements, and calming the negative effect of stress on the body are just some of the benefits of mindfulness.

I found I benefited enormously from accepting I was not my thoughts. The thinking process is ongoing; it's not something you can stop. Believe me, now that you've started interrogating the validity of your thoughts and the thinking process itself, you will be challenged. It's darkest before the dawn. Once we become consciously awake, we're tested—that's how it goes. To be awake is not yet to be awakened. My mind sometimes strides too far out into the future. When anxiety sets in, I succumb to analysis paralysis. The more I analyse and agonise, the less action I take.

Get ready—life is action, not thought.

Be Bright, Be Brief, Be Mindful

- Our inner monologue impacts our sense of ourselves and the world.
- Sometimes we forget that *we* are the ones listening to the negative mind chatter.
- Thoughts create, whether they are expansive or destructive is up to you.
- We can only consciously pay attention to one thought at a time.
- Mindfulness permeates through all aspects of being.
- Consciousness is not limited to the brain.
- Understand physiology and its impact on change.
- Exercise, name your clans.
- Be mindful of what you broadcast and receive.
- You broadcast energy and when you tap into momentum you can speed up that energy.
- Alignment = feel good. Out of alignment = feel bad.
- Yes, mindfulness can help you lose weight, but favour the term *gaining health*.
- Limbic System deals with emotions and memory. It is also where our involuntary or unconscious and endocrine (hormone) functions are regulated.
- Trust your gut – it is also intelligent and the seat of hormonal production.

- The starting point is awareness—being able to realize a situation is starting.
- It's hard to gain clarity of thoughts when your inner critic has the floor.
- Give your inner critic a moment to describe to you how it sees itself.
- Where are *you* in relation to your mind?
- The inner critic is a collective noun for a range of voices.
- Deep understanding and acceptance supersede language.
- You are neither your body nor your thoughts.
- It's not just inner mental critics. Our bodies communicate with us, too.
- Life is action, not thought.
- Mindfulness will help you be kinder to yourself and others.
- Practice the kindness exercise.
- By habitually rehashing the past and rehearsing the future we steal away the present.

Chapter Four Meditation
Look Who's Talking and Who's Listening

Welcome, and thank you for taking the time to practice mindfulness as you continue your journey through Mind Over Natter. We meditate on who's talking and who's listening!

We set our intention at the start of this meditation:

- We recognize at times we've allowed voices to run riot in our minds, ceaselessly talking, criticising, judging, and commenting. We acknowledge we're the ones listening and often internalise those thoughts.

- We are willing to engage in mindfulness, to quieten all the inner voices, and to listen to the silent wisdom of the divine within us.

As you get comfortable in your seat, on your cushion or lying down, gradually allow all the energy of the day to begin to slide off your shoulders. Feel the thoughts and worries of the day melting away and move out of your mind and into your heart space.

If it feels right for you, allow your eyes to relax either half open or closed. Relax.

As thoughts arise, that's okay. Acknowledge thoughts and don't try to stop them from floating across your mind, but don't allow thoughts to pull you out of this meditation.

Moving deeper into meditation, we notice our awareness might still be located outside of us. Our minds are still thinking about people, places, and plans. It's all about what's going on out there. Allow yourself to drop into awareness, staying peaceful. Drop down into your heart. This is not your physical heart but your heart centre, located in the middle of your chest. Feel warmth and love emanate from this area! Let the warmth and love envelope you.

If you stay mindful, the thoughts will slowly drift away just as easily as they drifted into your awareness. Use an anchor to stay mindful, bring your mind back to your breath, or a sound in your environment.

Breathe in. Breathe out. As you breathe in, give your eyes permission to relax, do the same with your mouth. Let your mouth relax into a soft smile. Notice the softness in your lips, and relax your tongue.

Breathe in, and take your awareness to your ears. They've been listening to thoughts drifting in and drifting away. Just take a moment now to thank your ears for all they do. Let your ears know you appreciate them. Send relaxing energy to your ears, and encourage your thoughts to let your ears have a rest for a few moments. Become aware of your ears relaxing. Enjoy the quiet.

We are soon emerging from this meditation. Your ears will feel refreshed and rested. Your mouth will feel relaxed.

Stay peaceful, keep your body still, breathe in deeply and release. Breathe in again, but this time, hold your breath and then slowly exhale.

When you are ready, and in your time, open your eyes. Take a deep breath, and release this meditation.

We fill our heart space with gratitude. Thank you.

May you be healthy, wealthy, loved, and happy.

CHAPTER FIVE
SELFIE TIME—AM I REALLY NOT GOOD ENOUGH?

> "If you are willing to look at another person's behaviour toward you as a reflection of the state of their relationship with themselves rather than a statement about your value as a person, then you will, over a period of time, cease to react at all."
>
> Yogi Bhajan

Good Enough

Waking from sleep that was good enough.
I'm alive in my life that is good enough.
The love I share is good enough.
How am I?
Who am I?
I'm good; and it's enough.

Selfie Time

I'm a "multipreneur" because a bunch of things interest me. I didn't want to commit to one and not enjoy the others. Many people these days have a range of business interests across a variety of industries. Others work a couple of part-time gigs at variable shifts, depending on what's available. It's the way the world is. We're no longer single-career to retirement. We don't even know what industries will exist in the next decade. In addition to my work in the field of mindfulness, I'm an author, a presentation skills trainer, a breakfast radio DJ, voice artist, singer, a multi-media content producer and presenter (including marketing videos, photography); I'm an MC, and keynote speaker, a Laughter Yoga leader and teacher plus I'm a tour guide. A lot of the work I do is on a volunteer basis, and as my self-worth grows, I've been able to ask for compensation, because I've realised I'm worth it!

As a tour guide, I get to show people around amazing places. I've learnt a tremendous amount about people and the assumptions they make, but something I wasn't anticipating was tourist selfie death.

Would it surprise you to know many people accidentally kill themselves taking selfies? A 2018 study of news reports showed between October 2011 and November 2017, there were 259 selfie deaths reported globally, with the highest occurrences in India, followed by Russia, United States, and Pakistan. [1] Luckily nothing so dire has ever happened on my watch, but I do get a teensy bit anxious at one of my locations—a rope bridge suspended between a cliff edge and an islet. It spans 20m and is 30m above the rocks below. I have to repeatedly warn visitors to be careful about backing up to the edge of the cliff when taking selfies. The walk to the rope bridge takes you down the cliff face and there are numerous selfie opportunities *en route*. Sometimes, these are riskier than the actual crossing. The point I'm trying to make is that we're used to taking images of ourselves, but we aren't used to taking inventory of ourselves.

The selfies in this chapter pertain to your self-image—not your physical self, but rather the way you perceive yourself to be. Who are you as a person?

Ever been likened to someone but you don't get the comparison? When people ask you, "What kind of animal would you be?" Can you easily relate to a creature that exemplifies your qualities? I introduce these ideas as an invitation for you to look at yourself and describe who you are. Many people battle with this exercise because they don't have a "relationship" with their identity. When people hear a recording of their voices, they're usually disappointed by the way they sound. How about taking it a step further? Let's go beyond what you look like, how you sound, etc. What does your mind look like? How would you describe the quality of your mind? Our whole world is processed by the mind, but we seldom contemplate what the mind is, where it is, how it works, and whether the opinions it has or the information it renders are accurate or not.

*Is your mind,
benevolent, ambivalent, or belligerent
to you and others?*

#mindovernatterbook

Selfie time—let's look at the mind from the heart's perspective.

Self-worth

Two qualities frequently highlighted by my clients as areas in which they need help are self-worth and self-confidence. When self-worth and self-confidence are negatively perceived they become silent killers that permeate our thoughts and inflict tremendous pain. Who says we aren't good enough? Who said it first, and have we believed it ever since? Many of us have internalised what we "heard" as our truth, and so we believe we are intrinsically not good enough.

People first assume they have a confidence issue, but after some introspection, realise the root of their pain is a lack of self-worth. Self-worth is a sense of one's own value or worth as a person. The Cambridge Dictionary defines self-worth as, "The value you give to your life and achievements. Many people derive their self-worth from their work."

Self-worth in terms of work, friends, finances, status, or the clothes you wear, is NOT the self-worth I am talking about here. *Mind Over Natter* challenges you to move away from comparison and competing and delve deep into your psyche, where your authentic self-worth resides.

What Determines Self-worth?

Self-worth is more about who you are rather than what you've done, or what you own, or what you wear. It's a sense of self that relates to values rather than valuables.

Societal conditioning has made us uncomfortable with any phrase that includes the concept of self. We're afraid to be perceived as vain or selfish, but there is enormous value in understanding who we are, how our mind formulates our thoughts, and then, how it responds to those thoughts.

My mind used to set a trap, and when I'd fall into it, my mind condemned me. I truly thought I was worthless, useless, and unlovable. I was the nowhere child with a bully for a mind. Once I stopped searching "out there" to find an authentic way to identify and bolster my self-worth, I began to hear the quiet inner voices of kindness and compassion. An important part of developing self-worth is the awareness for the need to change.

Our inner critics don't give us credit for changing, growing, developing, or enhancing our experience. Instead, they perpetuate the negative belief cycle that has plagued us throughout our lives:

You're stupid.
You're no good with money.
You don't know the first thing about accounts.
You'll always be a fat nerd.

Our inner critics also speak in first person, and that's why we tend to believe what's said, because we're the ones saying it:

I'm stupid.
I'm no good with money.
I don't know the first thing about accounts.
I'll always be a fat nerd.

Being mindful: stopping, breathing, assessing and only then responding allows us to interrupt this automatic cycle. Being mindful helps us accept that our thinking is outdated and more often than not, untrue! Our inner critics might remember incidents where we acted stupidly, but we aren't stupid *per se*, and many creative solutions are birthed out of error. The real problem is getting stuck in the negative cycle and then promulgating it.

An expansive sense of self-worth encourages us to look at situations more mindfully, more compassionately and more light-heartedly. We don't collapse at a problem; we start to look for solutions and remain open to possibility. Marie Forleo says, "Everything's figureoutable." If you feel you aren't good enough, any difficulty is ammunition to wound yourself again, which confirms the self-fulfilling prophecy.

Let's start by talking a little differently to ourselves!

Our thoughts change, as does our resistance. Instead of being a hostage to the inner critics, it's possible to welcome them and review their doubts and concerns to see if they have a point. As you raise your game, the critics will do the same, so you have to remain vigilant. Offer compassion to yourself and your inner critics, and that will change the inner atmosphere of your mind. Make your mind a place where change is accepted and acceptable. Opinions held by inner critics can change. We aren't stuck with a finite set of inner critics trapped in the past. We can shift them, change them, not believe them. They aren't easily persuaded, but with persistence, gentleness, kindness and compassion, they will change. They will become your allies instead of your enemies.

A nay-sayer can become your champion. Remember, not all the voices are negative—there are some affirming, kind-hearted ones who want you to believe in yourself as much as they do.

Although Calamity Knockherblock leads the Calamity Clan, instead of resisting her, I embrace her clumsiness and chuckle at her *faux pas*. She's an horrendous typo queen too, you can't imagine the things she's mistakenly texted. By relating to her from a distance and not strongly identifying as the *fumbling eejit* Ragnar Ragemeister (rage) labels her, I can regroup faster.

Self-worth & Self-esteem

Self-worth and self-esteem are intrinsically linked. Self-esteem is how we evaluate **ourselves**. It is an internal investigation of our qualities and attributes. When we challenge our negative inner critics with mindfulness a healthy self-esteem will start to develop because what we think, feel, and believe about ourselves is honest and realistic.

When you have low self-esteem you operate from a place of, "I'm not good enough." Everything that happens in your life is filtered through that deeply held notion, even though it is definitely not true. So even mundane interactions, once they go through your filter (your inner critics), can end up hurting you.

Self-worth is about knowing, and absolutely believing that you are worthy and valuable regardless of how you evaluate your qualities. In other words, if you have hit rock bottom and feel like shit, your self-worth holds onto the truth that you are still innately worthy! Are you worthy of another person's attention and love? YES. Are you deserving of receiving good things? YES. Do you have enough to offer other people so that they might value you? YES.

Just because you don't feel good about yourself, doesn't mean you're no longer valuable or worthy. That's why it's important to create a strong sense of self-worth to help you stay mindful when your self-esteem fluctuates, and believe me it will fluctuate.

We can't search for self-worth "out there". We don't find our worth by judging or comparing ourselves to others. It's an internal investigation and an absolute knowing that self-worth is intrinsic.

According to research by Jennifer Crocker, PhD, a psychologist at the University of Michigan's Institute for Social Research, college students who base their self-worth on external sources (including academic performance, appearance, and approval from others) reported more stress, anger, academic problems, and relationship conflicts. They also had higher levels of alcohol and drug use, as well as more symptoms of eating disorders. The same study found the students who based their self-worth on internal sources not only felt better, but they also received higher grades and were less likely to use drugs and alcohol or to develop eating disorders. [2]

Since the habit of judgment is thieving our joy, isn't it worthwhile to pay attention to the way our minds operate? Observe the thoughts you're having. I find the majority of my inner dialogue isn't nearly as sophisticated as I'd believed. My mind is not engaged in deep, cerebral cognition, but rather, it's nattering along repeating the same phrases today as yesterday.

Exercise: Name That Thought

Sit for few minutes with your journal. Start this exercise with the intention of identifying and naming your thoughts. What thoughts are running rampant in your mind right now?

Sit for the next five minutes, watch and then record, using a single word, what thoughts float in and out of your mind.

Your mind might be resistant to this exercise; that's fine—write down *resistance*. If your mind starts thinking about things you have to do later, then write the word, *plans* rather than describing the actual details. The object of the exercise isn't to write a stream-of-consciousness but rather to identify the different types of thoughts your mind is creating. If you develop an itch on your face or on your body, write, *body sensation*. If your mind starts getting anxious about the exercise or about plans for later, write, *anxiety*. If you hear something or feel something, write, *sound* or *feeling*. If a feeling comes up, write *emotion* or get closer to the meaning and describe it: *happiness, doubt*, etc. If you notice your breath in between the moments of awareness, write down, *breath*.

Your exercise might look like this:

Doubt
Resistance
Curiosity
Plans
Body sensation
Sound
Breath
Anxiety
Plans
Body sensation
Judgment

Selfie Time—Am I Really Not Good Enough?

Memory
Breath
Plans
Plans
Feeling
Judgment
Hunger
Frustration
Irritation
Painful knee
Memory
Memory
Breath
Breath
Acceptance
Curiosity
Quiet
Calm
Breath
Present
Sound
Plans
Plans
Distraction
Headache
Anxiety
Plans
Memory
Breath
Breath
Quiet

How did you find the exercise?

The list might be longer than this after five minutes. I wanted to show you how fascinating it is to see where your mind goes and what it thinks about. It's very hard to face our thoughts and to interrogate their ramblings, that's why so few of us do it!

Change your thoughts to change your life.

You can only change your thoughts if you know what they are. Mindfulness will reveal the quality and tone of your thinking. This is an opportunity to identify where the mind is placing its attention, and then shift or change it if that's what you'd prefer.

You don't have to rate yourself, and it's best to not berate yourself. Just be yourself.

How to Build Self-Worth

Seduced by comparison, many of us mistakenly define our self-worth by our net-worth. Strip away all the noise of the material world—achievements, acquisitions, accolades—and focus instead on awareness. **Awareness is key**. Identify which thoughts and feelings are your own and which were handed to you. With ownership comes responsibility. Upholding an opinion means being responsible for the consequences, good or bad, expansive or contracting. Identify what **you** truly think of yourself. Sometimes, our low opinions of ourselves come from people who had low opinions of themselves. It's not easy to clear the clutter to see what's true. Truth in itself is changeable, since we're perpetually evolving. What was true in our teens may no longer apply in our thirties.

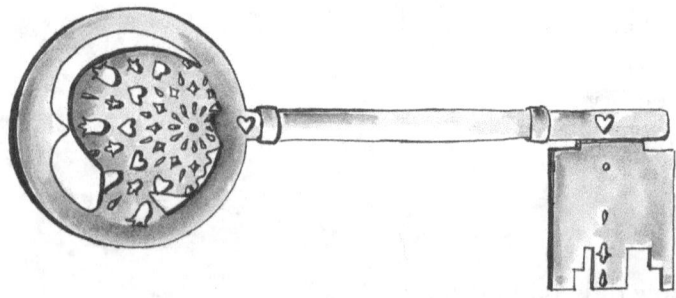

If your thoughts have caused discomfort to you or others, it's time to change. Sometimes, we inherit a false view of ourselves because our self-worth is low; we truly believe we're unworthy and not good enough. Judgment directed inward is potentially more damaging than judgment directed at others. As soon as you notice you are judging or comparing yourself to others, your body will react with discomfort. Remember, our bodies tell us the truth more often than we realise. I pay close attention to body language since the subtle, barely discernible tells from the body give me much more information than spoken words. Tune in to your body language, identify almost imperceptible body sensations to get an assessment of where your mind is in relation to where your higher self suggests it could be.

Evaluate your thoughts. Practice the short naming exercise where you identify what sorts of thoughts are preoccupying your mind. Use awareness to stop being a slave to your thoughts: align your thoughts to suit your intentions and always remember you are innately worthy no matter what!

Silence the Negative Inner Critics with Objective Observations

We need to challenge our inner critics, not obey them. If they offer worthwhile advice, at least you can follow it consciously rather than being reactive. A muddled mind leads to further confusion, fatigue, and stress. Get used to objectively viewing the way your mind works. Resist the temptation to judge or criticise yourself. Instead, say things like:

> *Isn't that interesting, my mind gets stuck on judgments about ____.*
> *Feeling distracted*
> *What's really going on?*
> *Let me focus on something else.*
> *I've got a sick feeling in my gut, I wonder what's wrong here?*
> *I can see my mind doesn't know how to describe itself.*
> *There has to be something I like about myself.*

The Six Step Self-worth Boost Camp

Mnemonics use a pattern of letters to assist in remembering.

For Self-Worth, Think *Worthy*.

When you feel you're at the bottom, that's great because there's only one way to go: UP!

W — **What pleases you?**
Do what pleases you, and if that pleases others, that's great. But you no longer need to please other people.

O — **Outside, in.**
It's always an inside job. Don't blame external circumstances for how you feel. Regardless of what happens "out there", you alone control how you feel about yourself.

R — **Respond, rather than react.**
Become aware of responding rather than reacting. Ask yourself, *am I responding (mindfully) or reacting (mindlessly/unconsciously)?*

T — **Think before you act.**
Sometimes, we react automatically. Think before you speak. Awareness and compassion will help you respond rather than react.

H — **Happiness.**
When you create happiness for others, you achieve it for yourself. Your true value lies inside you—happiness comes from peace of mind.

Y — **You are still alive, so keep going.**
Continually develop your internal resourcefulness, knowing there will always be challenges but you've got a 100 % track record of survival so far, so keep going!

The Six Step Self-worth Boost Camp With Coach Tara Malloy

Self-Acceptance

Many of us battle with self-acceptance because we don't want to acknowledge our flaws and mistakes; we would rather they didn't exist. We're human and prone to making mistakes. Accepting this eventuality doesn't mean we condone or must repeat the same mistakes. Acceptance means we acknowledge our imperfections, and continue to be compassionate and kind to ourselves as we move away from what doesn't serve us or others, towards what does. Perfectionism is a disguise for procrastination.

When you practice unconditional self-acceptance, you offer a kinder opinion of yourself. By being compassionate about aspects of your personality you feel need improving, you can focus on the change rather than berating yourself of the *need* to change. Adopting a mindful mindset gets you out of the habit of ruminating and into a practical plan of action. We can't authentically love our foibles, and neither should we, but we can offer loving kindness to ourselves for having them. This attitude will help stop the mental nattering and provide an environment that's conducive to change. Now, we can put a plan in motion to do things differently. This is what self-acceptance looks like: to compassionately recognize what went right, what went wrong, and then to adjust accordingly. I said I wouldn't be cryptic about advice so here are four keys to unlocking self-acceptance.

Four Keys to Unlock Self-Acceptance

The Mnemonic to Help You Recall Steps for Self-Acceptance is: *Self.*

S — **So, this is me.**
I accept myself. I have good, bad, and ugly aspects. I acknowledge that this is who I am right now, and I acknowledge that if I choose to, I can lovingly change.

E — **Enough.**
I am enough. Whether I adjust or retain my thoughts and actions, who I am is enough, and I'm at peace with that.

L — **Love.**
I make an unconditional pledge to be more compassionate and loving to myself.

F — **Forgiveness.**
I forgive myself for all my fears, flaws, quirks, behaviours, habits, and qualities.
In a spirit of awareness and compassion, I choose to forgive, stop punishing myself, and act or *respond* differently next time.

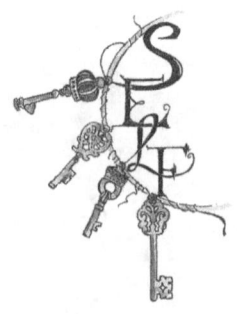

Self-Awareness

Many of us have an inaccurate sense of ourselves and it hardly ever occurs to us to update our self-image. It also doesn't even occur to us that we CAN. We happily update our technology without even questioning the merits of the update. We simply click okay, seldom read the terms and conditions, and then we click accept, and allow our devices to be over-written with updates. Is it not time for a self-awareness update?

What is Self-awareness?

Being self-aware is being able to *objectively* assess various aspects of yourself: your thoughts and feelings, your beliefs, words, actions and emotions, in accordance with a set of internal standards. The greater your level of awareness, the more objectively you can evaluate yourself. This enables you to manage your emotions so you can align your behaviour with those values and adjust if necessary. Self-awareness also helps you manage external conditions and the stress that arises from them. The quality and accuracy of your observations regarding self-awareness, is significant. If you assess yourself in a harsh way, you are unlikely to be objective. Being self-aware is to have a curiosity about what's going on inside you. It's looking for emotional blind spots, asking for feedback and being resilient enough to accept what comes up.

Self-aware people are able to monitor and observe their thoughts and feelings without attachment. They recognise mental patterns and can distance themselves from them by assessing whether they are true or accurate. Self-aware people seldom stagnate or get stuck in the past. Self-awareness isn't sugar-coating the negative aspects of our personality. On the contrary, it's about acknowledging what's *true*, being self-compassionate and then understanding the need for change. Self-awareness is not about judgement, rather it's about noticing and being willing to adapt. A hallmark of self-awareness is first asking questions of yourself and then finding answers and solutions, and lastly, taking the necessary action.

Exercise: Self-Assessment

1. Create a four-column self-assessment table like the example I've given below. What traits or characteristics do you like or dislike about yourself. (I bet the dislike list is MUCH longer than the like list). Every time I take groups through this exercise, people can't wait to tell me what they don't like about themselves. They find it harder to tell me what they do like. This exercise provokes resistance. Your inner critics are about to have a field day. Remember there are positive inner critics too, so let their voices be heard too, please. If it's easier for you to start with what you dislike, that's fine but we aim to balance the list and that's in our next point.

2. See how you can balance that list...see how TRUE or authentic the dislike list is and don't be afraid to own the truth in the like column.

3. In the last column, ask yourself, what action can I take, what can I change to become balanced and more authentic? If it's negative, what can you change? If it's a positive characteristic, can you enhance it?

Look honestly at the good, the bad, and the ugly (being mindful!) ...they all make us who we are... **no judgement**... but now you know the truth of who you are (i.e. self-aware) you can make the necessary changes. Acknowledge and celebrate the good things.

Selfie Time—Am I Really Not Good Enough?

It's not vanity to like good things about yourself. In fact, this exercise encourages you to enhance those.

To give you a broader perspective, include these subheadings in your table:

Personal, Mental, Emotional, Social, Physical, Spiritual, Traits, Characteristics

Self-Assessment Table.

The resistance that comes up in the like/dislike columns, points to an underlying factor that we need to address, and that is anxiety.

The Key to Unlocking Anxiety Is Mindfulness

Anxiety is prevalent in our thinking and throughout the world. Our minds are busy with thoughts about people, places, problems, pain, and our past. Quieten the noise and create a peaceful present through mindfulness. Mindfulness, enables us to actively participate in our lives rather than continuing to be a victim.

Anxiety rises when we perceive a threat or danger, and it doesn't matter if the 'danger' is real or imagined. The mere perception it might happen presents endless possibilities for the mind. We don't always understand why we're anxious. Often, we don't know we're experiencing anxiety since we haven't fully identified it. I call it the sick sense. We live with a sense that something is wrong. A multitude of worries flow in and out of our minds, through our bodies, and out into the world. Would you say that getting to know others involves getting to know their anxieties? How well do we recognise our own anxieties? Our lived experience of anxiety makes us familiar with its symptoms but not always its cause.

These are common anxiety triggers:

- public speaking
- meetings
- presentations
- divorce
- death
- illness
- moving house

- retrenchment
- retirement
- changing jobs

Anxiety often leads to fear, which in turn creates an instant body reaction: fight, flight, or freeze. We all respond to fear differently, but when in the fight, flight, or freeze mode, most feel threatened, trapped or debilitated. We react automatically, and we can't seem to shift psychologically or emotionally. We explode into often misguided reactions or we literally can't physically move. We can't see clearly or think coherently.

When feeling anxious or fearful all we want to do is protect ourselves, we want to hide instead of reaching out and connecting, because our mind draws us inwards and so we medicate, fixate, or intoxicate to numb the pain.

To address our anxiety on all levels, we need to expose the wounds to see what we're working with. We have unmet needs. When unmet needs become frozen needs, we develop negative limiting beliefs that trap and trigger us. We need to ask ourselves: *What am I really afraid of here? Are my fears real or imagined?*

Questions like these will draw your fears out into the open and when you shine a light on your fears it almost always halves your anxiety.

Exercise: So, what are most of us afraid of?

Fears activate the sick sense. We're interested in healing and transformation so let's explore your fears. I'll list a few, please add if you need to. In your journal, answer these points. What does it mean when you experience that fear? Draw an image of your fears. Things are always scarier in the dark, so let's shine a light on fears so we can face them.

1. Losing my job.
2. Losing my partner / parent / friend.
3. Losing my money.
4. Losing my house/ car / swimming pool (my status stuff).
5. Losing my health.
6. Being alone.
7. Never feeling loved.
8. Being perceived as a fraud.
9. Actually being a fraud!
10. Dying and not being invited to the after-party.

What do all of the above fears have in common?

Attachment!

When we create an attachment, we more often than not, make it the reason for our happiness and then we experience a deep fear of losing it. Many of our fears are well-founded but a great many more are either imagined or blown way out of proportion. Mindfulness reminds us we aren't trying to claim we're fearless, rather, we recognize fear, but we also notice we're actually fine despite the fear. Without mindfulness, we stay immersed in fear. We fear being alone, and so we develop unhealthy attachments which create anxiety around rejection, exclusion, and humiliation. When we attach to people, we mistakenly believe they'll make us happy. Our feelings of inadequacy and our lack of self-worth drive us to seek their approval and validation.

When we attach ourselves to money, we fear losing it. If we have loads, we want more, *just in case*. We think money will buy us safety and security, but this is an illusion. We think that when we're old, things will all be perfect, and we will be able to fulfil our whims and desires. We think we have time. We're so fixated on a future orientation; we aren't paying attention to the present moment. Our "vibration" (or energy) is all caught up in what we don't have; we unconsciously manifest more of the same. When we believe we aren't good enough, we attach ourselves to things or people hoping it will make us feel better. To make us feel good enough! Hands up anyone who's ever shacked up with a Narcissist and then thought you were the problem?

If we want to deal with our anxiety, we need to distil the anxious feelings all the way down to their core belief. It's not about making a moral judgment. It's more like seeing, observing, trying to understand what our mind is experiencing. What does it feel? What's it missing? What's it craving? What does it need?

To be in a state of wanting and consuming is a clear indication of attachment. If we want to fear less, we have to attach less. Fear is born from the attachment. It's a misconception to merely abandon attachment. When you embrace the present moment such as it is, you're letting go of attachment. By letting go of wanting things to be different, you attach less.

How many of us have bent over backwards to get someone's approval only to discover we're still miserable? Have you ever craved something, sacrificed everything to get it, then discovered it wasn't fulfilling at all? We can be loved and yet feel dejected at the same time. Mindfulness shows us that love for the sake of loving—not with a view to getting anything—is the way to experience non-attachment. When we love someone and genuinely want the best for them, we aren't projecting ourselves onto them at all. We aren't attached; we simply love them and want them to be happy.

Here's a poem I've just written about letting go of attachment.

The Letting Go

Fear grows in the mind that is afraid.
Life is loss.
I grip and toil
White-knuckle, close-fisted grasping.
Clench, wrench, I brawl, and haul
To the hoard, my needs, my wants.
Mine, mine, all mine.
I strive and strain but make no gain.
Life is loss.
Who am I?
The terror surge,
Shopping splurge,
Gone, all gone.
What next? What of me?
Forcing is false.
Let me let go.
Faith grows in the mind that releases fear.

REFRESH your SELF-IMAGE

How different would your life be right now if you could let go of attachment and simply press a refresh button? We're haunted by, stuck in, tied to, and shackled by our past. We carry the past with us in our minds, our bodies, our spirit. There's a saying on a wall at the Garrick Bar in Chichester Street, Belfast, Northern Ireland, that reads, "A nation that keeps one eye on the past is wise. A nation that keeps two eyes on the past is blind."

Staying stuck in the past makes us blind to the present and, by extension, the future. We spend the majority of our time gazing into memory and worrying about the future. If we are blocked by our belief in failure then we assume we have no choice and we feel trapped. Reframe that belief from failure to feedback. Feedback has an open energy, one that encourages a new pattern of behaviour: act, adjust, act, adjust, rather than the destructive, halting fear of failure which arrests future attempts to change. Feedback leads to a belief in the present moment effort. Feedback has an orientation towards the future since it restores choice and opens possibility. We feel more motivated to act, knowing we can adjust along the way, to get the results we want. Our tendency to operate on auto-pilot is problematic since we repeat past failures, and prevent ourselves from consciously living in the present moment. We spend our time reacting to external circumstance and not only does that make us a victim to whatever is happening, it detracts from our potential to make changes in the future.

We tend to romanticize or demonize the past, depending on how that serves our story.

#mindovernatterbook

Many people are fixated on a time in their past when they felt externally validated. Perhaps they were the popular kids at school or enjoyed success in a former career. They deny themselves the joy of the present moment by unconsciously trying to re-create the past.

Sometimes, we inherit from others the idea of who we are and that image may no longer be consistent with who we are now. Is your body image stuck in 1983, or when you were a teen, or in your 20s? Do you hear yourself saying words like, "never, seldom, probably, occasionally, often, always?" It's human nature to use these kinds of words to hold on to the past. We tend to romanticize or demonize the past, depending on how that serves the story we repeat to ourselves. Some of us are carrying deep-seated anger, resentment, and guilt rooted in the past which is destroying our present. These painful emotions were generated in the past, but their continuity is maintained in the present.

Update Your Self-Image

Your self-image is changeable: it's not cast in stone, and equally, it's not limited to your physical appearance!

I spent four decades loathing my body. She went everywhere I took her, ate everything I forced on her, and suffered my insults and mirror lambasting. Even though I poisoned her with sugar and carcinogenic fast foods and didn't take her out for walks, she still showed up. I didn't let her rest properly, yet I demanded she perform every day and criticized her when she didn't fit into clothes I hated. Why would *she* like them any better? I raged against her daily. Who does that? Unfortunately, many of us!

Our bodies reflect our thoughts. To change my body's image, I had to change my thoughts. I wouldn't treat anyone else so disrespectfully, yet I abused my body. I had to learn to actively avoid those hurtful and self-sabotaging behaviours and engage in healthy, compassionate, more loving ways.

Your self-image is the mental picture you have of yourself, both as a physical body and as an individual.

Exercise: Refresh Self-image

1. In your journal, write down what *feelings* come up for you when you think about yourself.

2. Without thinking too much about it, draw an image of yourself.

I know how uncomfortable this feels. The vulnerability's almost too much to bear. Introspection can be painful, that's why many of us avoid it. Yet, only when we look inside to discover the thoughts and feelings that are circulating, can we understand what's driving our behaviours, and creating our outcomes. If we want to make positive change, we have to put on our big girl panties (men too) and face ourselves.

Here's what typically comes up for me.

Unworthy
Lonely
Bitter
Unforgiving
Needy

What *images* come up?

Whether I'm ripped or rotund my self-image is FAT!
Weak jaw line
Bad hair
No eyebrows

Now, put your mindfulness glasses on and see what resonates as **true**, and what was created by others, or created by your negative inner critics? Once you separate truth from fiction, and you confirm there really are things you dislike about yourself, then that's great! Where you previously attached judgement and condemnation now you can release and make changes. If there is something you want to change, actively engage in *actions* that will produce your preferred appearance, or attitude and avoid things that will sabotage your efforts. It's as simple as that, but being mindful, compassionate and kind to yourself takes practice. Get out of your resistance-ridden mind and get into action where your body can contribute to the process. The present is the place to decide and act. The past keeps us trapped in memories that invariably become distorted. The future is the impossible zone. By all means work in the present towards the future, but denying yourself happiness right now for some future outcome that hasn't happened yet is mindless.

MEMORY: Remember + Feeling

The past exists in our minds, but we can change how we feel about it. Re-examine the way you interpret things that hurt you. You can recreate the experience and see it differently. Memory is often accompanied by a tainted feeling. We think: *It wasn't supposed to be like that.* This way of remembering forces us to hold on to sadness, anger, etc. Cultivate compassion and forgiveness for yourself and others.

*Forgiveness isn't about
the other person;
it's about you
releasing the attachment to the pain.*

#mindovernatterbook

Self-acceptance, self-compassion and self-love

Self-acceptance, self-compassion and self-love will help you change your perception of yourself. We are used to beating ourselves up with negative opinions that are mostly untrue. Being kind to yourself will help you develop a more accurate self-image in a more loving way. Profound changes are possible when you alter your perception of the past and of yourself. If you are full of self-loathing, you deny your own capacity. With self-acceptance and self-compassion, it's possible to nurture yourself through hardship. Self-love will inspire and motivate you to create and live a kinder version of yourself.

The way we perceive a situation can be reframed, and tone, meaning and context are adjustable. Let me expand. In a generalisation about someone at work you might have previously said: "She's such a nit-picking manager." Reframe this statement with kindness and compassion and see how the judgement changes to, "She's good at proof-reading where attention to detail is essential."

If you're anything like me, you have some self-loathing phrases on repeat. Start there. Clues to look out for? Remember when we were talking about the radio station of our mind, tuning in and receiving the signals that feel good or feel bad? You may have noticed many radio stations play music on repeat. These repeats are called high rotations and your mind plays extreme statements on high rotation like: *I always, I never* or *I'll never*. Reframe these with acceptance, compassion and love and you will be able to create a more positive atmosphere in your mind. Being self-critical is a habit. Judge less and look instead for ways to reframe those judgements. Your sense of self-worth will be enhanced by the kindness you offer yourself and others.

Top Tip:

If you find it uncomfortable, embarrassing, or just plain impossible to offer yourself acceptance, compassion and love, task your positive inner critics with the role.

#mindovernatterbook

Audrey Hepburn said, "Nothing is impossible, the word itself says "I'm possible!" Think about what that means. What could you do if you believed in your own possibility? Sometimes that's all we need, the vague notion that it's doable. People who achieve their dreams know that they need to nurture their bodies and minds as part of their journey to success. They see merit in speaking positively to themselves. Your positive inner critics are equally encouraging and supportive, allow them to support you with kindness until you can do it for yourself.

Quotes on Self-Worth

Buddha
"You yourself, as much as anybody in the entire universe, deserve your love and affection."

Mark Twain
"A man cannot be comfortable without his own approval."

Eleanor Roosevelt
"Remember always that you not only have the right to be an individual, you have an obligation to be one."

Louise L. Hay
"Loving ourselves works miracles in our lives."

Sahaj Kohli
"The fact that someone else loves you doesn't rescue you from the project of loving yourself."

Stacey Charter
"Don't rely on someone else for your happiness and self-worth. Only you can be responsible for that. If you can't love and respect yourself—no one else will be able to make that happen. Accept who you are—completely; the good and the bad—and make changes as YOU see fit—not because you think someone else wants you to be different."

Ram Dass
"Your problem is you're afraid to acknowledge your own beauty. You're too busy holding onto your unworthiness."

Sidney J. Harris
"It's surprising how many persons go through life without ever recognizing that their feelings toward other people are largely determined by their feelings toward themselves, and if you're not comfortable within yourself, you can't be comfortable with others."

Ralph Waldo Emerson
"Most of the shadows of this life are caused by standing in one's own sunshine."

George Eliot
"It is never too late to be what you might have been."

Suzy Kassem
"Stay true to yourself. An original is worth more than a copy."

RuPaul Charles
"If you can't love yourself, how the HELL you gonna love someone else? Can I get an AMEN?"

Maybe you have a favourite quote that helps you reconnect with your self-worth. Save it on your phone, make it a meme, write it in your journal. Use the power of those words to help you feel better.

Words are powerful and when they're put to music—they inspire superpowers within us! Music is central to everything I believe in: tapping into rhythm is like touching my own heartbeat, resonating with melody is like being in harmony with the sound of the Universe.

The DJ in Me Can't Help Herself

I've been a radio DJ since 1989—I truly believe music is life. I have an abundance of feel-good pop songs to recommend, but here is a quick-fire list of my Top 40 happy tracks.

Make happy playlists of your own. If your inner critics dispute the list, invite them to choose the music they love. Change genres—this is a pop list. I haven't even gone into musicals or Disney soundtracks, which also feel so good. There are so many other artists I adore, and I'm sure you do, too. Enjoy how the songs help you to press your refresh button to feel better.

Top 40 Happy Tracks

1. "Hold On," Wilson Philips
2. "You Are the Universe," Brand New Heavies
3. "Don't Worry, Be Happy," Bobby McFerrin
4. "Step by Step," Whitney Houston
5. "Happy," Pharrell Williams
6. "Raise Your Glass," P!nk
7. "Dance with Life," Bryan Ferry
8. "Holiday," Madonna
9. "I'm Coming Out," Diana Ross
10. "Ain't No Mountain High Enough," Marvin Gaye and Tammi Terrell
11. "Where Is It Written?" Barbra Streisand
12. "Catch My Breath," Kelly Clarkson
13. "Best Things in Life Are Free," Luther Vandross and Janet Jackson
14. "Moving on Up," M People
15. "Kiss of Life," Sade
16. "Firework," Katy Perry
17. "Something Just like This," Coldplay

18. "I Gotta Feeling," Black Eyed Peas
19. "Life is a Highway," Tom Cochrane
20. "Dignity," Deacon Blue
21. "Back to Life," Soul II Soul
22. "Change," Lisa Stansfield
23. "Freeway of Love," Aretha Franklin
24. "Feeling Good," Nina Simone
25. "Spotlight," Jessie Ware
26. "I'm Every Woman," Chaka Khan
27. "Sisters Are Doing It for Themselves," Aretha Franklin and Annie Lennox
28. "You've Got a Friend," James Taylor / Carol King
29. "Somewhere over the Rainbow," Judy Garland
30. "Let's Go Crazy," Prince
31. "The Lion Sleeps Tonight," Solomon Linda (under the title Mbube)
32. "Army," Ellie Goulding
33. "Club Tropicana," Wham!
34. "Reach Out (I'll be There)," The Four Tops
35. "Don't Stop Believing," Journey
36. "Spinning Around," Kylie Minogue
37. "Born This Way," Lady Gaga
38. "Don't be so Hard on Yourself," Jess Glynne
39. "Sweet Freedom," Michael McDonald
40. "Groove Is In The Heart," Deee-lite

When you're happy, you radiate happiness which feels good for you and this energy expands out into the world which is good for everyone and everything else.

Actively engage in positive, expansive thoughts, words, and deeds. Actively avoid negative and contracted thoughts, words, and deeds. Maintain this mental discipline, and your life will begin to flourish.

Selfie Time—Am I Really Not Good Enough?

 **Be Bright, Be Brief, Be Mindful**

- How would you describe the quality of your mind?
- Is your mind benevolent, ambivalent, or belligerent to you and others?
- Selfie time—look at the mind from the heart's perspective.
- The root of pain is a diminished sense of self-worth.
- Your self-image is more than your physical self—rather it's the way you perceive yourself as a whole person.
- Many of us internalise a moment and make it a defining belief that becomes our truth.
- Self-worth is more about who you are than what you do or have done.
- An inner critic, at best, is a point of view, a reflection of painful past experiences from early life.
- Over time, we internalise the inner critic's opinions and subsequently believe them.
- Being mindful helps us interrupt the automatic acceptance of the opinions upheld by inner critics.
- We can't add value to something we fundamentally believe to be worthless.
- Mindfulness is a practice that moves us away from judgment and back into moment-to-moment awareness.
- Change your thoughts to change your life.
- You can only change your thoughts if you know what they are.

- Emotions have a physical response.
- We can change how we view and feel about the past.
- Forgiveness is an act of self-compassion.
- Refresh and update your self-image.
- Mnemonic: W.O.R.T.H.Y. for self-worth and S.E.L.F. for self-acceptance
- Being kind to yourself will help you develop a more accurate self-image

Chapter Five Meditation
Selfie Time - Am I Really Not Good Enough?

Welcome, we meditate on refreshing your self-image and accepting you are good enough, just as you are.

We set our intention at the start of this meditation:

- We choose to give our thoughts the space to express themselves, rather than dismissing them. We acknowledge that the mind thinks, and that is okay. Today, we're going to observe what the mind is thinking and notice each thought and not try to change it, being careful not to judge it, simply allowing, accepting, and acknowledging thoughts.

As you are getting comfortable in your seat, on your cushion or lying down, gradually allow all the pent-up energy of the day to dissipate from you.

If it feels right for you, allow your eyes to relax in a downward-looking gaze, half open, or all the way closed. We hold a lot of tension in our eyes, forcing them to read multiple devices all day long. Give your eyes the opportunity to relax and let go. Send gratitude to them for all they've done for you today, and enjoy the feeling they offer as they relax and take a break.

Breathe in through your nose. Breathe in as deeply as your lungs will allow. Pause, and then slowly release the breath. Breathe in for a count of four. Breathe out for a count of four. Allow the breath to revitalise the body and refresh the mind. Enjoy the calm of your own breath.

Now extend the outbreath to a count of six. Continue to breathe in for four. Breath out for the count of six. A longer, slower out breath. Relax.

Now release the counting and just breathe naturally. In through your nose. Out through your nose.

As a thought comes up, label it with a single word. You might imagine writing a hand-written sticky note on the thought. Perhaps a light illuminates the thought. Some people like to attach a balloon to the thought. Maybe you simply see thoughts as words floating away into the sky. Let them drift out of your awareness, watch them dissolve to nothing.

If your mind resists this exercise, that's fine. Label that thought *resistance*. If your mind starts thinking about things you have to do later, then label those thoughts *plans*. If you develop an itch on your face or your body, label that *body sensation*, and let the thought go. If your mind says you shouldn't be labelling things, acknowledge that thought, and let it go.

The label is just a tool to help you unpack the activity in your mind. If worries or problems that have been weighing you down surface, label them *worry, problem, or anxiety.*

Remember: not all thoughts are negative, and you might even find a happy thought coming into your mind, label it *joy.* If you hear something, label *sound.* If a feeling comes up, and it is laden with emotions, label *emotion* or get closer to the meaning and describe it *happiness* or *doubt.* If you notice your breath in between the moments of awareness, label *breath.*

Take your time. If this is difficult, challenging, boring, or uncomfortable for you, then be compassionate and say, *I notice this is hard, and that's okay.*

Mentally say: *I am good enough.*

Notice what happens. If your inner critics argue, let them express themselves. Listen compassionately without interruption. Once they have finished, you can offer, *Thank you.* How different would your life be if you believed you were good enough? Review moments in your life when you did feel good enough. If your critics refuse to let you think of a time, take a moment right now and imagine what it would feel like to be good enough. Can you access what that might feel like?

Take some time now to explore the mind. Experience the range of thoughts that come up for you. As they arise, notice them and let them fall away. Breathe in through your nose and out through your nose. Invite thoughts, label them and then then let them go. Hold a space for the next thought. If it takes a while for the next thought to surface just breathe and be present.

We are soon going to emerge from meditation. Stay peaceful, keep your body still, breathe in through the nose, hold, and release. Deep inhale, hold, and long, slow exhale through the nose. And a third mindful breath full of purpose and control, breathe in steadily and slowly through the nose. Fill your lungs. And slowly exhale in a sustained, slow release through the nose. Empty your lungs.

Use these three deep breaths to calm you whenever thoughts tumble around in your mind. Mindful breathing will help slow the momentum of your thoughts. Mindful breathing will help shift your focus away from your busy mind!

Rub your hands together to create heat and place them over your eyelids. Once your hands have cooled, take them to the side of your face, almost create blinkers at your temples. When you are ready, slowly open your eyes.

Breathe in and release this meditation. Say silently or out loud if you feel comfortable, *thank you.*

We fill our heart space with gratitude. Thank you.

May you be healthy, wealthy, loved, and happy.

CHAPTER SIX
RESILIENCE—HOW DO I BOUNCE BACK?

"You are strong enough to face everything that life throws at you, even if it doesn't feel like it right now. You are resilient, and you can get through anything you put your mind to. Listen to your inner voice, and allow it to guide you down your path to enlightenment, Amazing blessings are waiting for you."

TheLawOfAttraction.com

Resilience

After my
        f
        a
        l
        l

I realized I hadn't failed
I'd merely lost my way
The way itself; wasn't lost.

After the tears

I realized I could laugh again
Benevolence smiled on me
I leaned in for the kindness.

After some time

I realized I could trust again
Comfort consoled me
I opened my heart and discovered

I was found.

Resilience

Resilience is about our mindset. Let me expand with this meme I saw recently:

~~Why is this happening to me?~~

What is this teaching me?

My negative mindset kept me trapped in precisely that victim mentality, asking *why me* rather than *what's this teaching me*? I went even lower with the classic, "Woe is me." Have you said that? Heard others say it? How does it make you feel? I can sympathise but truthfully, it frustrates me. It reminds me of my stagnation. I seemed more invested in staying stuck than transforming my way out of there. "Woe is me," feels so helpless and hopeless. Wouldn't it be cool to break free from being a victim and embrace opportunities to learn or improve?

Abraham Hicks suggest getting ahead of problems before they even arise. It's the next level in transformation and it gets exciting. Stay focused and tuned in to what you want because it's better to work towards something you want, and reduce your obsession with what you don't want. Clarity gives a sense of purpose and makes you more aware of potential problems that might arise. When you're out there being creative, you're not in your reactive mind. If you have clarity and emotional enthusiasm for a task, you are likely to attract more positive energy to contribute to its successful outcome. Life teaches us that problems inevitably arise. Abraham Hicks suggest in "The Vortex", that facing those problems is made easier through a single point of contact.

> There is no relationship of greater importance to achieve than the relationship between you, in your physical body, right here and now, and the Soul/Source/God from which you have come. If you tend to that relationship first and foremost, you will then and only then, have the stable footing to proceed into other relationships. Your relationship with your own body;

your relationship with money; your relationship with your parents, children, grandchildren, the people you work with, your government, your world…will all fall swiftly and easily into alignment once you tend to this fundamental, primary relationship first. [1]

You already have evidence of your vibrational alignment, your ability to be happy, to do what you love, and to enjoy that with others. So, when a challenge arises, you are equipped to meet it without losing your feel-good resonance. No matter how difficult a problem becomes, with practice and belief in your ability, you can offer steadfast resilience in body, mind, and spirit offering physical, mental, and emotional resolve. If a problem is an entanglement, get used to unravelling it and not allowing it to unravel you.

The way we respond to challenges sets up the tone and our identity for the next series of events. When facing a problem, if we become reactive and aggressive, we can be sure to draw in a range of negative complications that will undoubtedly expand the problem. So, be prepared. It's not that we should expect the worst, but rather, we should be ready, willing, and able to act when the worst arises. Stay ready to face whatever happens. Adjust your attitude towards problems. Instead of wasting frustrated, negative energy on them, choose instead to use the opportunity to test yourself. Rather than staying stuck in analysis paralysis, dreading problems and not doing anything, get out there and enjoy overcoming problems. Sometimes overcoming problems provides an unexpected turbo boost towards opportunities you hadn't even contemplated.

The Negativity Bias

Have you ever found your thoughts circling around and dwelling on an insult or found yourself fixating on your mistakes? Ten people praise you, one puts you down, who gets your attention? Criticism wounds, but many of us are uncomfortable with compliments. As psychologist and author, Dr Rick Hanson says, our brain acts like Teflon for compliments and Velcro for criticism. In, "Hardwiring Happiness," Dr Hanson explains how the brain evolved a built-in negativity bias.

> While this bias emerged in harsh settings very different from our own, it continues to operate inside us today as we drive in traffic, head into a meeting, settle a sibling squabble, try to diet, watch the news, juggle housework, pay bills, or go on a date. Your brain has a hair-trigger readiness to go negative to help you survive. [2]

My brain is hyper alert for negativity. When it doesn't detect any incoming, it has no qualms generating some on its own. I suffer with insomnia, and that's precisely the time my inner critics love the most. When I can't sleep, inner critics target me with their negative rants, lining up one awful memory after another, and they even remember things I'd forgotten. They don't limit themselves to the day's disasters, either. The more desperate I am to sleep, the more determined they are to dredge up some debacle from the past or some cataclysm that awaits.

Bad news frequently draws more attention than good. For some children, negative attention and being shouted at is better than being ignored. Do you have a punctuality problem? It's said that arriving late is a self-sabotage technique to gain attention. Negative events have a greater impact on our brains than positive ones. Dr Hanson explains this in terms of carrots and sticks (positive motivation versus negative motivation). If we're beaten to death with a stick, we can't exactly show up the next day to hunt for carrots. (Just checking in, did your inner critic chirp, *You don't hunt carrots!* You see what I've been saying? You can't even read in peace, without inner critics nattering along.) A negative stimulus has a more powerful effect on our behaviour, decisions, and our relationships since the activation could mean life or death. In pre-historic times, the part of our brain that evoked the fight/flight/freeze response had to be hyper-vigilant, otherwise, we might die or be excluded, which would mean death, only not before we'd endured loneliness, isolation, vulnerability, and abandonment.

To build up resilience, we have to identify how the negativity bias impacts our thought process. It can detrimentally impact our mental health when we focus only on what's wrong, or only concentrate on pain, and constantly dwell on dark thoughts. I have to carefully manage my inner critic, Darah McDark lest she drags me into her chasm of doom. She has the habit of justifying why things are so awful. She likes to recruit others to prove her point. Our thoughts tend to be negatively aligned, and it takes effort to reframe them and to overcome the negativity bias. It takes awareness to stop the negative self-talk of the inner critics. Instead of fixating on mistakes, integrate what they've taught you, and apply the lesson when your next challenge arises. Reframe the situation. Get used to questioning your inner critics and the views they hold about you, your past, your experiences, and the people around you. It's easy to jump to conclusions or be paranoid.

Instead of looking at things in a contracted way, see if you can reframe them more expansively. I'm not saying to break into a song and do a dance, but you can use mindfulness to assess a situation without emotionalising it. That said, a feel-good tune and moving your body may be just what you need to help you bounce back. Focus on what's happening, not on what you *think* or *feel* is happening, since sometimes our thoughts and emotions are inaccurate.

Develop your awareness on at least three levels: negative, neutral, and positive. What do I mean? We tend to think in extremes where negative events are perceived as bad and positive events are good. We don't even notice neutral events, and when positive ones happen, we seldom acknowledge them. Most of our growth emerges from negative situations. When we shift out of complacency, invariably an opportunity emerges. Our perception is that a negative event is bad and to be avoided but the reality is that negative events enhance our resilience. Napoleon Hill said, "That is one of the tricks of opportunity. It has a sly habit of slipping in by the back door, and often it comes disguised in the form of misfortune, or temporary defeat. Perhaps this is why so many fail to recognize opportunity." Obstacles open doors of opportunity and if you change your mindset, you can leverage the positive from the negative.

Remember to celebrate the good moments. Pay attention and focus on success and solutions so your resilience is rooted in learning from problems and celebrating solutions.

The Positive Contribution of Mindfulness to Resilience

It's fine to sit on a mat or go on retreats. Those are lovely practices, and everyone should experience a formal meditation practice. I think silent retreats are essential. However, it's not always on retreat when issues arise, so mindfulness needs to be integrated into everyday living.

We're on a journey and haven't arrived there, yet. *Happily, Ever After* simply doesn't exist. There's always a twist and a turn and an opportunity to experience contrast. Along the way, there will be evil witches, dragons, demons, trolls, and other archetypes of our making to overcome! Rough times happen and painful situations arise—there's no denying the challenges we will face. That's the beauty of mindfulness—it doesn't specify piety or blandness. It's an invitation to notice how we're behaving and from that awareness, make choices that lead us away from painful situations towards pleasant ones. Mindfulness is the bridge from pain to gain. Thirty-seven trillion cells listen to your thoughts because consciousness exists throughout the body. When you fully comprehend the power of your thoughts, you'll feel compelled to watch what you say, especially about yourself.

Honed meditation skills help when you're in despair, through heartache, and when you're feeling overwhelmed. You learn through meditation to move beyond your story. Mindfulness helps you become aware of what story you're telling yourself and others. Awareness encourages us to stay present in the now rather than what happened before or what's coming. By continued self-reflection through mindfulness, we can make space for new thoughts, new decisions, and new ways to act. We become less *story* and more real.

We can refresh our point of view and update our self-image when we discover that panic-inducing moments promote opportunities for us to adapt, change, develop, and thrive in our lives. Panic less, act more. When we see someone change their life around, we want to know their secret. Some of us don't give ourselves credit for having the same potential, and so, rather than be inspired, we succumb to jealousy and clam up, not even trying to change. Scarcity mindsets frighten us into believing we're somehow excluded from abundance. We doubt we can achieve a happy, healthy, fit, lean body, or create an income in a field we love. We think all the good ones are taken, and we're doomed to be single for the rest of our lives. Or, we tolerate a relationship we know is toxic.

Going Nowhere Slowly...for Ten Years

I went nowhere slowly for a decade after a sixteen-year relationship abruptly came to an end. I couldn't find my resolve to bounce back. I felt like I'd lost everything. She was the love of my life and my best friend. Our son enhanced our love for each other and we adored him. When he was little, we'd scoop him up in our arms, holding him in our embrace for a family dance. We became soccer moms as he grew older. In fact, parenthood introduced us to some incredible people at parties, sports events, school functions, concerts, etc. Once we stopped thinking of other mothers as the "carpark mafia," we began to feel less threatened and could open up to meeting new people. Not everyone accepted us, but that's life.

[*1]The end of our relationship meant an end to the extended relationships of family and friends. We weren't married but I always thought of my former mother-in-law as my second mother. My sister-in-law and her husband, and their children—were equally precious to me, and still are. I didn't want my son to suffer the anguish of a broken family as I'd suffered when my parents divorced. When our relationship ended, I felt like my whole life imploded. In fact, I probably contributed to the continuing collapse in all other areas of my life since I was so acutely aware of loss, pain, and suffering. The situation did indeed worsen, and this is key—things will go from bad to worse unless you do something about it. I capitulated and the energetic vibration I offered was loss and suffering, so that's precisely what I attracted:

- My health deteriorated; I became gravely ill.
- My employment contract wasn't renewed.
- My agents ditched me.
- Friends ditched me.
- I ditched some friends too as I felt too ashamed to face them.
- I moved house a few times.
- I sold my fancy car and bought a cheaper one, then sold that one at a massive loss to try mitigate my financial blundering. I bought another, cheaper car, and my ego was horrified and humiliated that I had to drive in what my inner critic, Snoot, described as a *tin can on wheels.*
- I signed ridiculous contracts that cost me a fortune.
- I was a wreck.
- Everything I touched turned to shit.

[1*] True at the time, but thankfully those relationships and the one with my ex have been restored.

The list goes on …

I was floundering. I could have done with seeing this meme, "If you feel you're losing everything, remember that trees lose their leaves every year and they still stand tall and wait for better days to come."

Wishing, willing, hoping, dreaming, and intending are great starting points, but they all require *action* to start you moving towards manifestation. The metaphor I used at therapy was that I was falling down a grease-lined well. I was plummeting in the darkness to some unseen horror. Who knows what was at the bottom since clearly, I hadn't reached it yet. I couldn't get a grip and stop the fall since the walls were so slippery. I felt like a victim, and I acted like one. I was deeply entrenched in my misery. I stopped going to therapy. It never occurred to me to reach out for help or be gentler with myself. I believed it was impossible to regain control of my life. The critics went for the jugular. I became suicidal.

One night, driving the car Snoot detested, I was stuck in my thoughts and not watching the road and I drove onto a sandy embankment. The loose gravel thrust me into a violent spin. A part of me thought, *Oh I didn't mean that,* and another part of me thought, *Oh, well, you wanted to die, so if you go like this, at least it'll appear like an accident.* I recovered the car in plumes of dry dust, my headlights shining particles into a golden glow. Cars drove by, unaware of the life and death battle I was waging against myself. Ordinarily, I'd have taken the situation as a sign that my problems were illuminated as insignificant as dust—I had the wheel and could choose where to direct my life. Instead, the incident opened a diatribe between my clans. Some of my inner critics were baying for blood. They thought I surely had to be worthless, *After all, weren't you left standing, stunned at the airport curb side, watching your love of sixteen years literally walk out of your life?*

I succumbed to a morose melancholy that lasted for years. I couldn't speak about my love loss without tearing up. I tried to be brave for our son who wanted me to be stronger. When I say I was depressed for a decade, I'm not exaggerating. The best I could manage was to offer the appearance of being alive in my life. Somehow, almost osmotically, I began to absorb the teachings of mindfulness and meditation. I ventured into relationships—one was a hazard. The next one might have been lovely, but we triggered each other and couldn't get past our pasts. There was one, almost moment but my inner critic, Sab O'Tage, destroyed it before it got going. I never should've attempted the one after that, and then I met someone in Northern Ireland, and after a year and a bit, we got engaged. Then, we broke off our engagement, and after five months, reunited and re-set our engagement, complete with an engagement party and detailed wedding plans. We went venue-hunting, selected our theme, made food and entertainment choices, but we didn't make it. I thought I was taking action, allowing myself to live and love again, but like a swan, I suspected I only loved once. That's just a story I was telling myself. Relationships need clarity and cohesion—of course we can all love again, start with yourself then see about someone else.

Sometimes, we get clear on what we want after a bad experience that emphatically shows us what we don't want. Hands up anyone who's tried internet dating only to discover that prospective partner should have stayed in the cyber world? What about faithfully pursuing a career only to discover your hobby is more aligned to your personality, more lucrative, and far more likely to survive the next recession than your 9 to 5 job?

A healthy dose of resilience is fundamental to an enjoyable life. People often say they want life to be smooth-sailing, but what we really want is the strength, courage, tenacity, and sheer grit to overcome heavy seas. Since life is all about ebb and flow, crests and troughs, we can trust our experience will reflect those ups and downs. When I used to cycle ultra-distances, coming to a series of hills was always daunting, but on the positive side, I could see there were fewer hills to climb once I'd conquered the first, plus I could race as fast as possible on the downslopes.

As for my personal plummet, I restored balance through spirituality, mindfulness, meditation, music, movement and laughter.

I howled, then laughed then howled with laughter. I showed up laughing as a daily practice, like an exercise programme. I cried tears. I grieved. I forgave. I leaned on the love of Mother Father Creator, my sister's enthusiastic support, a sense of protection for my son, encouragement from family and friends, and the love of my two dogs, Rhiley and Keegan who (like my mother) have passed but still strengthen me.

My heart was literally broken, and at forty-four, I had a dual chamber pacemaker inserted. After arduous training as a triathlete for Ironman, I learned I had anomalies with my heart. A couple of years before, I relocated to a coastal town and met an amazing friend who owned a SCUBA diving school. I qualified as an advanced diver, shot an underwater movie for her dive school, and we started triathlete training. Initially, it was only for the fun of it. Then, we were bitten by the Ironman bug and fully submerged ourselves—body, mind, and soul—to endless swimming, cycling, and running. The race director grounded me after he'd heard of my collapse in the pool during swim training. I went under lengthy heart investigations, which highlighted the need for a dual chamber pacemaker. I had to abandon my life as an ultra-athlete and de-train in order to give my heart a chance to heal.

Ailments!

After heart surgery, I developed extreme, chronic pain and was diagnosed with Fibromyalgia and Chronic Fatigue Syndrome. For years, I'd suffered with Endometriosis and eventually had to have a hysterectomy. There were complications with that surgery related to my pacemaker. I had liver problems as a child and meningitis as a teen. I suffer with severe headaches to this day.

The arthritis in my neck, caused what's termed an "inverted neck." It's painful and has exacerbated the headaches. I have limited movement through my body with widespread joint and muscular pain. My back, pelvis, hands, feet and hips ache every day, making life difficult. For years, I had to sit on a special cushion because coccyx pain was off the charts. Even a short car journey was excruciating. I have Eosinophilic Esophagitis, which presents as a strange kind of choking that's inconvenient at best, potentially fatal at worst. On more than a few occasions, I thought it was tickets. I have allergies of all kinds, especially to cats and pollen and wheat. I have lung issues, and sometimes, the wheeze is so loud I disturb meditation classes. I had surgery on my knee after high-impact sports damaged it. It's never been the same, although I did do Kung Fu afterwards. I have sciatica in my right leg. I struggle with poor sleep, and my bowel is so irritable I can barely manage to get to the loo on time. It's hard to fend off depression when I'm so acutely aware of a multitude of physical pains.

The depression after my pacemaker was next level. I recognised I needed the machine in my chest, but I simply couldn't get my mind to accept it. Each time, I could feel it working to restore my heartbeat, instead of being glad to have it, I felt like I was being monitored and manipulated by technology. I joked this wasn't the Ironman I'd intended. People asked to see the scar, or they noticed the swelling under my skin. They made squeamish faces. What's that about? How was I supposed to respond to that? I tried to make light of it, but secretly, the machine in my body wasn't a joke. I was frightened of it, and it made me feel disconnected and strange. In the first few weeks, I couldn't lie on the left side of my body as the machine had to embed. It felt uncomfortable and painful when it squished into the tissue in my chest.

I took the ailments of my body, heart, and mind into prayer and asked for help to handle the pain. Though I'm in pain to this day, I've learned to stop fighting against it and lean in towards it instead. I don't disregard the pain but I accept it is here, and that lessens its impact on my life. I use my experience with pain to offer empathy to others.

I studied mindfulness, Laughter Yoga and cognitive behavioural therapy, and I did everything I could to overcome my anxiety. I qualified separately as a Mindfulness Teacher and Laughter Yoga Leader and somehow, helping others with their suffering took me out of my own. Resilience, for me, was a daily demonstration of showing up, despite mental, physical, and emotional pain. Even though I was choking and aching, I was doing a photoshoot, presenting a radio show, filming a video, or teaching a presentation skills, mindfulness or laughter workshop. There are always people who've suffered worse or gone through greater tribulations. It's not a game of who is worse off. I recognise each of us has a journey that's uniquely experienced. What happened matters less than how we respond to it. I stopped phrasing things as "my ailments." In the same manner that we stop identifying with thoughts, I actively worked at not identifying with pain. Our next action impacts how we feel now and how we can expect to feel in the future.

Your Burning Desire

Before we explore the "bounce back" strategies I'm about to offer, I'd like to help you get crystal clear about what Napoleon Hill calls *your burning desire*. I used to think a burning desire was a blazing passion for something. Hill's version, refers to burning your boats so that you commit to the landing. You desire what you came for so greatly, that you're prepared to stay, invest, and destroy your escape plan. In the past, I've been accused of a lack of commitment. It stings when someone else says it, but I know it's true—sometimes I'm just not that invested. Maybe you've been non-committal or indecisive. Did that uncertainty cause you additional frustration because you just didn't know what to do? If I hesitate, that tentative feeling often leads my negative inner critics into a chorus of:

> *You're weak!*
> *Make up your mind!*
> *Not this again!*
> *Analysis paralysis!*

I'm so worried about making the wrong decision, I don't make any decisions. Feeling stuck makes it worse. Life can't be sustained in stagnation, it needs movement. To live at an optimal level, we need to cultivate decisiveness. Total commitment doesn't mean inflexibility, it means you're all in and if you need to change, then change. It's not greedy or selfish to commit to living your best life—there is abundance for everyone. It takes resilience to return to the quest when you've lost your way, and it takes motivation and then action to reset and carry on. Fear atrophies our action muscle. Develop a habit of making decisions and acting on them swiftly before doubt sets in. If they don't work out, make new decisions and act differently. If you cling to an escape plan, you're aligned with the way out not the way forward. Motivate yourself with a clear picture and strong feelings of achieving your desire rather than envisioning disaster.

Motivation is a subject that deeply fascinates me because we each experience it so differently. Most of us know what we don't want, but are we clear about what we *do* want? The Spice Girls ask a good question in their song *Wannabe*, when they ask: "So tell me what you want, what you really, really, want?"

What do you want *in* your life, *from* your life, *for* your life? Have you ever articulated it? Phrase it positively, not negatively. "I don't want to be in debt," still references debt. Say, you'd like to have extra cash available, or disposable income after your bills have been paid. If this is what you want, get clear and express it clearly.

If you feel uncertain about how to describe your preferences, begin with some common categories:

Work
Finances
Spirituality
Health
Relationships
Love
Family

Then there are some more subtle areas:

Purpose
Contribution
Healing
Environment

Exercise: Clarifying What You Want.

Get your journal out, make pie charts, draw doodles, make a vision board, get creative, and have fun.

1. What do you want?

2. If you aren't sure what you want, give yourself a mental hug. Resolve to continue the exercise even though a part of you thinks it's stupid, and you want to throw this book away once and for all. Resistance is an indication that you've touched a nerve, and you're on to something—your emotions are agitated, and they need freedom to express themselves. You can even say to yourself: *Other people also feel this way.*

Many people have felt this way and get frustrated with this exercise, and here are some actual responses from my clients:

"It's not my fault."
"I don't know what I want, just not this."
"My father said, *You made your bed, now lie in it.*"
"I'm stuck."

"I'm not saying that I blame my mother, but in a way, I blame my mother."

"I've been putting out fires for so long, I haven't a clue what I want."

"It doesn't matter what I want."

"It's just not realistic to go thinking about what you want when there's the rent to pay."

Play the Opposite Game for Clarity

There are many other despondent and downhearted comments people make. Our thoughts get us into trouble sometimes. So, even if your life is on the brink of breakdown, that means you are a significant creator. You thought your way in, now think your way out. It's time to create what's good for you now instead of manifesting the stressful life you've generated up until this point. The opposite game takes any scenario and says: *What could I do to mess this up?*

Let's say you've started a list that says "new job," but you don't know what you want beyond that. Play the opposite game and ask the question: *What could I do to mess this up?*

- I could show up late.
- I could dress inappropriately.
- I could be disrespectful to the customers.
- I could take an advance and spend all the money even before I've earned it.
- I could drink/take drugs at work.
- I could damage their company car.
- I could disregard their policies and not check in or check out for work.
- I could badmouth them on their social media.

- I could bitch to others and get them agitated about management.
- I could take leave before I was due any time off.

3. Run through your list of what you want. Expand some scenarios asking the question, "What could I do to mess this up?" A clue here: just review your fears. You've already worried about messing up so tap into your fears and get them out of your head and onto the page. From think to ink.

4. Next, ask yourself, "What could _____ do to mess this up?" Now you put yourself in the perspective of "the other" and run through scenarios of what they could do to mess this up.

Continuing with the example of "new job," here's what the prospective employer might do to mess this up. Again, this is what you imagine they might do, you've already worried about it, now we're just looking at the fear physically written down. This is empowering. Facts seem less frightening than fiction.

- They could make me work late and not pay me.
- They could insist I wear a uniform that I have to buy.
- They could be disrespectful to me, especially in front of colleagues and even in front of customers.
- They could pay late or not at all.
- They could condone an environment of alcohol and drug abuse at work.
- They could expect me to use my car for company business and if it got damaged, not compensate me.
- They could tie me up in unreasonable policies and procedures.

- They could badmouth me in the industry.
- They could scheme towards my constructive dismissal.
- They could deny me due leave.

So, when you wrote down "new job," and felt you didn't know what you wanted, with a handful of minutes and a modicum of effort, you've got much greater clarity. You played the opposite game to learn what you *didn't* like. Now, see how it looks when you turn your energy towards defining a positive and enriching work experience.

As a result of the opposite game, there is a bit more clarity.

- I work reasonable hours for good pay.
- Whether I wear uniform or clothes from my closet, it is my choice to dress for success.
- I work in an environment that promotes self-respect and the respect of colleagues and clients.
- I'm paid regularly, on time, and with a clear breakdown for tax purposes.
- I work in an environment where clear thinking helps us excel and where none of us feels the need to rely on alcohol or drugs.
- Whether I use my transport, public transport, or company transport, I arrive safely, on time, and in comfort to do my work.
- My workplace has useful systems to make it easier for all of us to know what's happening.
- I work in an environment where people use their words carefully.
- I work at a place where everyone feels validated; a place we enjoy working in together.

- When my leave comes up, I'm happy to take it as I enjoy holidays. I value replenishing my energy, and I'm confident I will return to a positive work environment.

5. Take other categories and play the opposite game with them, too. Make lists of what you don't like in order to flip them around to what you do like. When you consider what you don't like, be as negative as you like. Really get down and dirty. Then, transform those ideas into positives. From your new positive list, create overviews, make plans, set goals and create affirmations that deeply resonate now that you can fully align with them since you've banished doubt and escaped fear's grip.

Thoughts Are Powerful, but Feelings Are Even More So!

If you have areas you want to work on, and I haven't listed them, you can create categories that pertain to your life. Get clear on what you want in each one. Remember, thoughts are vibrations, but feelings have even stronger vibrations, so use your thoughts to create powerful emotions. Feel the emotions rise in your body. Sense the physiology of positive emotions and focus more on those rather than the sickening feeling you have in your gut when you are worried about something. Set timelines for your vision in each category. Offer a time limit to make it more feasible because a goal remains an intangible dream when left without a finite date.

Focus on your burning desire. Remember, you aren't looking to escape, you're committing to expand. Later, you can set an action plan. You might not know *what* to do at this stage. You might not know *how* to do it. The how trips us up when we bring it in too early. At this stage, it's really useful to focus on how it would *feel* if your dream came true. It's important to know *why you want this*, so don't get bogged down by *how you'll get it*. Maintain that high vibrational feeling in your body, of how it would feel to achieve your goal. Increase positive emotions when you visualise your burning desire coming true. This is a limitless feel-good time so let your imagination run wild with everything good that you want. Go big, and ask yourself: *Why* are these items on my burning desire list? *Why* are they important to me?

When you have your *why*, then try and understand what the why *feels* like. Get that feeling into your body and fully experience the surging, positive, expansive emotions. Get excited—jump, run, and shout. It's like you can barely contain the enthusiasm. You'll have even more clarity when your body also participates—enjoy it and make it fun. Move. What've you got to lose? You've already experienced a life of pain, so how about creating one of possibility? This *feeling* will help motivate you, keep you resilient when the journey gets tough and setbacks happen. If you have a clear why and you know how good it feels in your body, you feel more connected to it and less likely to let it fall by the wayside. Now you are ready to take some small action. Give yourself time. Start with what you have, and build from there. Once the universe sees you've made up your mind, it will conspire to help you.

Mental flexibility will help you to navigate any obstacle, hindrance, or interruption. Instead of allowing frustration, disappointment, or anger to well up inside you, it's wiser to expect challenges and complications. Notice they might be pointing you to a better way, or a change of plan that could benefit you. At all times, your happiness matters. Don't only grant yourself happiness when you complete a task or reach a goal. Happiness is the magic state that makes everything possible, the secret sauce. Get really interested in what it means to be happy!

Why Happiness Matters

Whether you are on the path for the first time, about to bring a burning desire to fruition, or finding your way back after a setback, your happiness is important. Why wouldn't happiness be a priority? What's the sense of misery for misery's sake? I spent too much of my life being serious. Where is it written that we must all live solemn, sombre, stony-faced, unsmiling lives? Even writing those words makes my mouth turn down. Happiness feels right for all the right reasons. It's physiologically good to laugh; it's great exercise, and it releases stress-busting hormones, and there's always someone with a peculiar squeal or shriek to push you on for more.

For my forty-first birthday, I threw a party with a difference—I hired a laughter yoga coach. Instead of an evening meal and drinks, I made it brunch at a restaurant where we cleared the tables to make space for the silly sessions. It was the best thing I could have done for my friends, many of whom were executives striving for high-powered positions but sadly heading for ill health induced by stress. I underestimated the way people would respond to the "chortle aunty"—some were dubious, some were outright uncomfortable, literally hands up, backing away and shaking their heads at her laughter invitations. She got them all laughing, and we still talk about it today. If there's a laughter coach at a conference, book that session. Laughter and happiness aren't the same thing, but they pair perfectly together, and when we integrate them more into our lives, we live better, give better, feel better, and are better. William James said, "We don't laugh because we're happy, we're happy because we laugh."

I rediscovered the delightful practice of laughing for no reason when I bought a book called *Laughter Yoga* by the Giggle Guru, Dr Madan Kataria, the creator of Laughter Yoga. When Dr Kataria pointed out that most of us leave our laughter to chance, it struck a chord with me. There is increasingly less to laugh at in a world struggling with pandemics, wars, greed, poverty, global warming etc. and I knew my resilience depended on my ability to tap into the psychological and physiological benefits of Laughter Yoga. Laughter Yoga blends playful laughter exercises with deep yogic breathing and grounding exercises like Yoga Nidra. I immediately qualified as a Laughter Yoga Leader and trained with Dr Kataria himself in the art of laughter as a volunteered daily practice independent of jokes, comedy or humour. I did Business Laughter Courses, Laughter Yoga Therapy

Courses and I will shortly graduate from a Laughter Yoga Leader to a Laughter Yoga Teacher ha ha! Just reading ha ha! – makes me laugh out loud.

Ask yourself a few questions about what happiness means to you.

Meditation practice will help you to gain answers as you become a conduit for messages from your God, the universe, your higher power etc. If it's clarity you seek, deeper questions bring deeper answers. Real breakthroughs happen while in deep, inner contemplation and they can also happen in the midst of deep belly laughter that helps you release toxins of all descriptions. Seeking happiness outside yourself is a recipe for disappointment, but it's where most of us start. We think we want millions in the bank, lavish mansions, luxury yachts, etc. Yet, we all know mega wealthy people who're miserable. Happiness, like self-worth is an inside job. We experience happiness through peace of mind. I'd rather have peace of mind, that leads to genuine happiness, and *then* go for a spin on my wet bike launched from my private yacht! When you enjoy the external *through* your happiness, you're not expecting it to be the *source* of your happiness. Yes, I do think we can enjoy abundance, and I'm not suggesting peace of mind happens remotely on a barren mat. It happens each time we choose it.

If attachment means we're working against what we desire, striving for happiness has the same effect. Happiness as a pursuit is a misconception. To pursue or to chase something means it is always running away or elusive at best. It's not something or someone who makes us happy, happiness is an experience we enjoy inside ourselves. Very often, our happiest moments are in creating happiness for others and then delighting in their joy. We love by genuinely wanting the best for them, and when we create happiness for others, purely for their enjoyment, without condition, we also experience happiness, almost as a by-product.

So, how do we bounce back and be happy, healthy, wealthy, loved, and loving? These things alone don't always equate to happiness. Decisions are powerful and effective depending on the strength of your motivation. In each moment, we create a cause and experience the effect. This is why I emphasise vigilance with your thoughts. You could be so close to a breakthrough or to manifesting your dream job, relationship, etc. but it could all fall away at the last second because you allowed doubt to sneak in and change your thoughts. Our mind is the creator of our current and future reality. So, what you're *thinking* now is important to your present state and your future self's reality.

How to be Happy?

From my Top 40 Happy Tracks, Jessie Ware's *Spotlight*, has a powerful lyric, "Can't keep the air we're breathing." Happiness and freedom from suffering is like breathing, we can't keep them, we have to let them go. Some of us are addicted to our suffering. If you want to be happy, you have to let go of unhappiness. Care for your future self. Do you want her to be happy? How do you think she'll be happy? Her happiness is like yours, a choice. Your future self can only be happy if you lead by example now. Like Dr Kataria said about laughter, don't leave your happiness to chance.

Imagine taking the suffering away from your future self. Isn't that an incredible prospect? Wouldn't it be an amazing investment? Dreams do come true. Happiness is possible. Keep your thoughts fixed on what you want and watch, with delight, how they manifest. We're not expecting to be happy all the time. Life is more colourful through light and shade. We live in a creative, abundant universe, and when vibrations align, things happen. Magic happens. Unfortunately, we've perfected the art of self-perpetuating our negative thinking. The good news is, we can manifest happiness, but the bad news is, we keep manifesting unhappiness. The Law of Attraction suggests "that which is like unto itself is drawn". You already have evidence of it working against you, now get it to work for you.

So, how do you bring all this into a real, lived experience for increasing happiness?

- Move your body.
- Cultivate mindful awareness.
- Regular meditation at least morning and night, increase as you go.
- Voluntarily laugh for ten to fifteen minutes a day.

If your image of happiness is a successful relationship, then begin to cherish other people's happiness and patiently deal with compassion when difficulties arise. If you are nagging less, judging less, and less paranoid, it makes you so much easier to be around. Consider who you are in a relationship and how you treat your partner. Would you enjoy the way you speak to them, the expectations you have of them? How are you speaking to yourself, and what personal expectations do you have? Our capacity for growth increases over time, but only when we become more trustworthy of ourselves. When we trust ourselves to give the kind of love we would like to receive, we literally vibrate an energy that will be equalled.

You will *attract* people into your life that have the same vibrational energy you have. Your energy will align with their energy and you will have literally created a genuine connection, whether it is within an intimate, business or friendship setting!

A To-Be List Rather Than a To-Do List

Would you like to see a different kind of to-do list? This is a to-be list. It's a short list.

Filter everything through these two concepts to be happy:

Be compassionate
Have a peaceful, positive mind

*We don't use expressions like
getting happiness
or having happiness;*

we talk about ***being*** *happy.*

#mindovernatterbook

One day, I had tourists from around the world with me on the coach. It had snowed overnight and was chilly the day of our tour. One of the ladies continually moaned about the cold. We had the heaters on full blast but she continued to complain. When I sat down beside her I could plainly feel the heat emanating from them. She was ruining the atmosphere for everyone, but more than anything, she was making herself glum. I used every ounce of compassion I could muster to keep serving her. At one of the stops, I offered to take a photo of her, but like a determined ice queen, she glared at me admonishingly and snarled, "Stop being positive." I showered her with attention the whole day, but her review was: "Informative and enjoyable tour ruined by the cold in the bus." Her happiness was entirely up to her.

Resilience – What's Important

Resilient people experience more happiness. You might not think you are particularly resilient but you have a one hundred percent success rate for bouncing back. We often get caught up in regret, and we undermine, underestimate, and undervalue the courage we've shown to survive to this moment.

Resilience is about the story you repeat. Is this an obstacle or an opportunity? If you are firmly rooted in a compassionate alignment, you can easily reference care in any arising situation. Care for what's happened, who's affected, and what can be done. It gives you a problem-solving mentality rather than allowing yourself to remain stuck.

Resilience is about recognising that "shit happens". How we respond to it makes all the difference to our future selves and to those around us. What is your intuition advising? The sooner we act, the sooner we diminish the chances for our inner critics to tell us this is impossible and we're all doomed.

*Be conscious of thoughts
that boost or burden.*

#mindovernatterbook

Spirituality

What does it mean to be spiritual? Spirituality is different for everybody. Being spiritual doesn't mean being religious. In childhood, our parents or caregivers may have imposed their religious beliefs on us. Learned theology and ideology, imbued with a sense of obligation, may lead to renunciation. Sometimes it's the religion that rejects us and sometimes we reject it. Religions follow sets of rules, regulations and rituals. Perhaps your inner critics highlight levels of religious hypocrisy, corruption and political interference, whereas zealots find ways to justify these.

Mythologies in different regions account for variable creation stories that devolve into a separation between humanity and a creative energy. Some express a connection between a Deity or deities, while others correlate with the cosmos. Certain tribes are strongly aligned with the ancestors and follow oral traditions. Others believe in the power of nature and place significance on seasons and animals. There are beliefs in magic and supernatural powers. For some people, there is no creative thread weaving anything together—there's no special meaning to any of it.

Before we get too entangled, here's singer, Bonnie Raitt's take on spirituality, "Religion is for people who are scared to go to hell. Spirituality is for people who've already been there."

You'll have heard the phrase that we are spiritual beings having a human experience. We can agree we are all human but hardly any of us agree on our spiritual beliefs. This fundamental disagreement is the cause of untold conflict throughout history. The Buddha said, "The Way is not in the sky; the Way is in the heart." The Dalai Lama's view is, "Love and compassion are the true religions to me. But to develop this, we do not need to believe in any religion." An Apache prayer says, "Looking behind I am filled with gratitude. Looking forward I am filled with vision. Looking upwards I am filled with strength." An African proverb describes the spirit of collective contribution, "It takes a whole village to raise a child."

Does spirituality suggest there is a link between who we are, and what we do? In Hinduism and Buddhism, Karma is the sum of a person's actions in this and previous states of existence, and it's viewed as deciding their fate in future existences.

There are as many beliefs as people, so I won't quote from every tradition and I haven't even introduced science yet.

Maybe I pressed some buttons at the mere mention of science, religion and spirituality. Martin Luther King Jr, said, "Our scientific power has outrun our spiritual power. We have guided missiles and misguided men." If my guidance doesn't serve you, I respect that. If my suggestions are worthwhile, the best that I can offer, is that you exercise discernment in everything. If certain philosophies no longer resonate with you, discard them. Choose what inspires and uplifts you. Perhaps the essence of a spiritual life is using free will appropriately. To cherish others and to develop self-compassion sounds a lot like, Jesus Christ saying, "Love your neighbour as yourself."

You have a bigger system under your command than you may have realised—you're coordinating body, heart, mind, and soul. To boost my resilience, it really helped me consider that I have the Mother/Father Creator supporting me—and that despite decades of assuming it, I've come to believe it's impossible for me to be alone. When I tap into the power that is simultaneously part of my essence and the essence of the universe, I feel sustained with strength and the impetus to go on—my life becomes significant, miraculous and wondrous. You are the captain on the bridge, whether sailing on the ocean, flying through deep space or navigating the vast expanse of your mind.

Some Resilience Questions To Ask Yourself

What would I like to:

- Put down
- Pick up

- Hold
- Be

Resilience involves letting go and it can also mean holding on under pressure. Being tenacious is a mindset and then a behaviour. Resilience comes in all shapes and sizes: sometimes it's determination, sometimes it's being stubborn. Our fortitude is frequently tested. Waft almond-flavoured cupcakes near me and my resistance might buckle. We're familiar with trials and tribulations, but sometimes, resilience is about simply holding on to the vision of our heart's desire. We have items on our bucket list that seem important and dramatic. Bucket lists are important, but we spend far too much time "wishing", and not enough time actually doing in our day-to-day to get those items on our list. Become invested in the day-to-day.

What could you put down? A memory, a grudge, an unrealistic goal? How different would your life be if you could only put that down? If there's something you've always wanted to pick up but haven't done it yet, do something to pick it up. How about learning Ballroom and Latin American Dance? Always wanted to play an instrument? Learn a sport? You should start to feel excited when you think about your heart's desire. Start by researching: online then in person. Ask others, let people know. Go to places where you can see these things happening. Eventually, if it's something you love, you'll pick it up for real.

If you have something you hold dear, and you've compromised, then re-establish that connection. Maybe you've held on to a value or an aspect of your personality that you've protected despite all sorts of attacks. That's beautiful. Cherish those qualities. And who would you like to be? This is a question we all struggle with. It's the ultimate question—only you can answer! Only you can create the person you want to be in spite of your past. You have immense power – and it's within your grasp to envision, design and manifest the best version of yourself.

Bounce Back

Our spiritual practice matters, and through meditation we can feel more supported by Universal energy. Who would you be if you knew you couldn't fail? Have you ever actually bounced on something? Wasn't it fun? The word, "bounce" even sounds like fun. It's almost onomatopoeic isn't it? B O U N C E. Resilience is having fun with problems, not making problems worse. Bounce back. There's an element of energy in there. Bounce back into the situation ready to make it better. Play more, lighten up, don't take it all so seriously. I'm not saying be disrespectful. I'm not denying your pain. Try being frisky about stuff. When I suggest that to people, they just about recoil in shock. Why not be frisky though? A playful attitude, even in the midst of a serious situation, can help lighten the load. I really walk the talk on this one. In fact, I created a dance with a song I wrote called "Laugh it Off!" It's about laughing off free-floating hostilities and not taking it all so seriously tee-hee!

A few years ago, I made a documentary about cancer survivors describing their lives after surgery. One woman had been through liver cancer and breast cancer with all sorts of complications and heartache. All she wanted, was to see her son get through school. She had a sleep over for him on his birthday. There were a bunch of kids sleeping in the lounge, and one of the kids (a sleep-walker) bumped into the TV. In the commotion, she sprang from her room to check everyone was alright. She'd forgotten to grab her wig and the kids were frightened when they thought it was Uncle Fester who'd run into the lounge. She began to laugh, and they laughed with her, not at her! Her willingness to laugh at herself and the situation *created* a safe space for the kids to let go of their anxiety and laugh with her. She bounced back even more by humming the Addams Family theme tune as she got them all back into bed.

 ## Be Bright, Be Brief, Be Mindful

- Resilience isn't always about picking yourself up. Sometimes, it's about avoiding getting knocked down.
- When you're out there being creative, you're not in your mind being reactive.
- Our brain acts like Teflon for compliments and Velcro for criticism.
- In order to build resilience, we have to identify how the negativity bias is impacting our thought process.
- Resilience is composed of learning from problems and celebrating solutions.
- When challenges arise, mindfulness equips you to meet them without losing your feel-good resonance.
- The way we respond to challenges sets up the tone for the next series of events.
- By continued self-reflection, through mindfulness, we can make space for new thoughts, new decisions, and new ways to act.
- Thirty-seven trillion cells are listening to your thoughts. Consciousness exists throughout the body.
- Wishing, willing, hoping, dreaming, and intending are great starting points, but they all require aligned action to start moving towards manifestation.
- Sometimes, we get clear on what we want after a bad experience that emphatically shows us what we don't want.

- What *do* you want in your life, from your life, for your life?
- Play the Opposite Game for clarity.
- Thoughts are powerful and feelings even more so!
- Happiness and laughter matter.
- Create a *to-be* list.
- Cherish others and develop self-compassion.
- Transform the mundane into the meaningful.
- What would I like to:
    1. Put down
    2. Pick up
    3. Hold
    4. Be

Chapter Six Meditation
Resilience - How Do I Bounce Back?

Welcome, and thank you for making the time to care for yourself in this mindfulness meditation on resilience and how to bounce back. These meditations have been created especially for *Mind Over Natter*.

We set our intention at the start of this meditation:

- To practice resilience.

Make yourself comfortable on your chair, your cushion on the floor, or lying down. Wherever you are, gradually allow yourself to come into this moment. Let go of the tension that has built up in your body. Leave behind the worries and troubles of the day and just surrender to this moment as you sit and breathe.

Drawing in your focus, aware that your mind is still producing thoughts, become conscious of your presence inside your body. To help your mind slow down, if it feels right for you, close your eyes and be less involved in the world "out there". Notice your breath. See what's going on in your mind and your body. There's no need to change your breath at all, but quietly see how your body is breathing at this moment.

We all have tendencies to want to change how things are. Just acknowledge this thought. Just breathe and let go of any expectations you might have. You don't have to do anything else. Enjoy the calming sensation of the breath as it slows and deepens.

Feel your body letting go. Enjoy what that feels like when you start to relax your body. Gradually, you're slowing down, your breathing is slowing, your body is slowing, and your mind is slowing down, too. Notice how light your breath is. Your body only needs to draw in soft, light breaths. Release them slowly and let go gently.

Notice the sounds in your environment. Notice the vast space between you and the sounds. Expand that awareness out further to the edge of the room, to the outside of the building. Imagine the space above the building, beyond the clouds, through the stratosphere, beyond the planet, further out, way out, passed the galaxy, out, into the depths of deep space. Consider everything in this vastness is full of kindness. What would it mean to you to be surrounded by kindness, compassion, and understanding instead of negativity, hardship, and cruelty?

Know that your mind is just as expansive. Fill your mind up with kindness, and expand that feeling outwards. Your mind has enormous space, no fences, no boundaries, no walls!

You've shown incredible resilience already. Remember a few recent examples of your inner strength where you stood true despite the pressures you faced.

Continue to relax. Allow the breath to revitalise your body and mind. Everything is as it should be for you in this moment. We habitually give ourselves a hard time, and we don't give ourselves enough credit for all the incredible things we do; even just showing up each day takes a lot of effort. Acknowledge your courage. Notice what that feels like in your body—first, the feeling of courage, then what it feels like to be acknowledged for being courageous. Spend a moment in that space.

We're emerging from meditation. Inhale through your nose. Exhale through your mouth with an "Aaaaah" sound like making a gentle sigh. Breathe in deeply and breath out, "Aaaaah."

We recall our intention at the start of this meditation: to contemplate resilience. You have overcome a great many challenges and in taking the time to nourish and nurture yourself through this meditation, you are growing your intrinsic resilience. The more you do something, the easier it feels, and the greater your confidence grows. Consistency boosts capacity. Breathe in, and acknowledge your resilience. Exhale, knowing you can expand it further.

When you are ready, and in your time, open your eyes. Breathe in, and then exhale and release this meditation.

We fill our heart space with gratitude. Thank you.

May you be healthy, wealthy, loved, and happy.

CHAPTER SEVEN
GO FOR IT!

"It is impossible to live without failing at something, unless you live so cautiously that you might as well have not lived at all."

J.K.Rowling

Go for it!

The settling of my glitter-globe mind,
Shows me—
It's possible
I'm possible
Yes!
Feelings bubble up.
I'm moving, I'll keep moving
I'll go for it!

At the beginning, I spoke about your life being all about belonging and connection and that I hoped reading this book would bring you into a new phase of genuine happiness, optimal health, love, purpose, and abundance. I hope you feel more akin to the tribe and know you're not alone. We all have a journey that involves meeting trials and tribulations and overcoming them with resilience. It's time for you to shine. I've always been intrigued by the journey of light that shines from the stars. Jeanette Winterson captures that fascination so eloquently, "Look up. This is the season of shooting stars. Light, two thousand years old, still dazzling. Let me see your face. Your face lit up by twenty centuries." I encourage you to look up and lighten up and become familiar with reframing the negative into positive. Be curious. Have fun. Laugh more. Your happiness matters.

Updating your self-image is fun. If you like something, keep it and expand it. If you don't, change it, start where you are. Be fastidious with negative critics—your own and out there. Give them limited attention just long enough to take their feedback and make your adjustments. Don't internalise their cruelty. If there are setbacks, learn from them, implement changes as they arise, or simply resolve to do it differently. Even self-sabotage can have a positive spin—we learn how powerful our old habits are, and we get a fresh look at the changes we want to make. Create a clear vision of your life then live into it.

Be aware that your body is constantly changing as is your mind—it's learning, adapting, and integrating—something it will be doing for the rest of your life. Listen to your intuition. Meditate. Write Morning Pages, as suggested by Julia Cameron, author of "The Artist's Way." Write three foolscap pages of uninterrupted, unfiltered thoughts, first thing in the morning. They're the primary tool for your creative recovery.

> We are victims of our own internalized perfectionist, a nasty internal and eternal critic, the Censor, who resides in our (left) brain and keeps up a constant stream of subversive remarks that are often disguised as the truth. The Censor says wonderful

things like: "You call that writing? What a joke. You can't even punctuate. If you haven't done it by now you never will. You can't even spell. What makes you think you can be creative? And on and on.

Make this a rule: always remember that your Censor's negative opinions are not the truth. [1]

I had the privilege of meeting Julia Cameron when she was giving a writer's workshop in Birmingham, in the United Kingdom. I had to circumnavigate my negative critics who were cringing at the thought of me daring to ask her a question. I remembered what she'd said about the "Censor" and so I took the microphone and asked in my creamiest DJ voice, if it was:

A) Better to get back to pages later in the day (if you didn't have time to write the full three pages)

B) Skip altogether and pick up the next day

C) Write what you can first thing, even if it's a single page or just a paragraph.

Her answer was: C. It's better to write what you can first thing, even if it's just a page. Her point is that writing pages gets us out of our own way. It's almost as though pages become therapy as well as advice. Sometimes pages help you get the negativity out. Also, you can't keep moaning about the same thing. Eventually you'll be compelled to act.

All that angry, whiny, petty stuff that you write down in the morning stands between you and your creativity. Worrying about the job, the laundry, the funny knock in the car, the weird look in your lover's eye—this stuff eddies through our subconscious and muddies our days. Get it on the page. [2]

Writing Morning Pages the other day, this phrase came to me:

Align your objectives for the day before your objections set in.

#mindovernatterbook

Julia said writing later in the day about *gratitude* is a different energy and an equally worthy exercise in clearing the day and recognising what was good about it. Pages are private. Don't read them to people and don't allow others to read them without your permission. They're meant to be unfiltered so you can get your deep, dark, troubling thoughts out of you in order to lighten you up for the day. This is an opportunity for your inner critics to fully express themselves. Keep a separate journal for pages, and another daily journal where you can create, play, and be colourful.

Use everyday mindfulness to create health, wealth, love, and happiness. Find reasons to be grateful for people, places, pets, the planet, moments, and events. Remember to rest and relax but also to play a bit more. Get a bit frisky. Play more happy tunes. Be active. Move your body. Be grateful for all it's done for you so far, and listen to its wisdom. Offer it nutrition, hydration, exercise, rest, and kindness. Enjoy yourself. Laugh more. Explore new ways to experience what being alive feels like. Comfort zones are complacency traps, so get out of there!

We complain about having to go to the gym. Some people don't have a gym contract. Some people don't even have legs to move. I saw a wee dog today with only three legs. My heart was full of compassion. The dog didn't need my sympathy. He was out and running, and he didn't let his missing leg cause him to miss out on life. Have you ever seen a dog arrive at a park and moan about not having enough time, being stiff or bored? Dogs don't stand at the entrance, berating their owner for not bringing them often enough. Dogs don't nag about wanting to have been there earlier. They don't focus on wanting the conditions to be different. They don't feel like a victim if they're the only ones at the park, or if its crowded, or that the other dogs sniff their bums too enthusiastically. You can take a dog ten times for a walk or a run, and even if they're sick, they'll move because they feel compelled. Life moves through them; they're present-moment aware, and they enjoy it.

Go for It!

Love. Be loving. Love more. I want to encourage you to have a *go for it* attitude. The phrase implies action, with clarity and focus. I didn't say set off tentatively when the conditions are absolutely perfect, when you've lost ten pounds, when you have romance, when you've got the job of your dreams, when you win the lotto, or when you have perfect health. I said go for it – NOW!

Try not to multi-task. Focus on one thing at a time, and stay in alignment with it until it comes into manifestation. There's no hidden doubt. Get the doubts out: from think to ink. Banish greed; it's no good, it's scarcity in panic mode. Sometimes we have to just get over it before we go for it. What do I mean? If you are so focused on the past, lugging it about, sustaining the pain, it's really hard to go for it. I saw this delightful image of a Unicorn farting some rainbow gas and the caption was, "Sometimes you've just gotta let that shit go." My other favourite is a diva collapsed over a couch saying, "I'll get over it, I just need to be dramatic first." I'm not being cavalier about letting go, I know how hard it is when you've been hurt. You can't climb the ladder and reach for the next rung if you don't let go of where you are. Being blocked is tough. Staying blocked is worse.

Sometimes, going for it means researching first. Going for it might involve strategising, but don't get too caught up in plans. Get used to taking some small, aligned step in the direction of your burning desire. Be patient—going for it doesn't mean you've got it yet. It means you've started, and that's a good thing. I always used to say to my son before he went out, "First, have fun, and do no harm." If your task is arduous, don't dwell on the awfulness. Go for it, and get it done. If you are unsuited to a certain line of work, there's no point in going for it. The same is true with relationships. Don't go for a "Get rich quick" scheme offered by some slick, hot-shot. Use the vigilance you have within you to verify if it's a viable opportunity.

A summary about the chapter on self-worth is that it's an inside job and you are enough right now.

All manifestation starts with a clear vision of what you want, then aligning your thoughts, feelings, and actions to create your objective.

Go for it; even if you have nothing, you can still conjure up feelings of what it would be like to have your burning desire. Get clear on what you want, feel positive, have faith it will come, take the necessary action to support it, allow time, receive it, and then remember to give thanks.

Acknowledge who you are right now—a child of the universe surrounded by abundance. With self-compassion, choose to refine your self-image, and go for it knowing you already are everything you'll ever need. You are a human being, not a human having or a human getting. As writer, Florence Scovel Shinn, says, this is the "Game of Life." She cautions though that our imaginations are powerful tools, and that whatever we send out in word and deed is returned to us, "If he gives hate, he will receive hate; if he gives love, he will receive love; if he gives criticism, he will receive criticism; if he lies he will be lied to; if he cheats he will be cheated." [3]

Look for the good in any given situation, and when a negative one arises, address it promptly. *Don't get stuck believing your beliefs.* Remember, you aren't your inner critics. Hear them but make up your mind. Make decisions. If they don't work, make new decisions, but don't be a fence-sitter. Commit. Go for it if you have a dream that lights you up. Go for it if you want to transform your life. Go for it if you feel your nutrition needs revision or you want to move your body more. Go for it if you think a different career would be good for you and your family. Go for it if you want to train in martial arts, to grow edible plants, to develop a craft, an art or a hobby, to get into motorsport, to learn animal training, to volunteer … the options are endless. Go for it!

Gratitude is a beautiful quality and so is generosity. When we feel grateful, we feel less hateful. When we feel generous, we enjoy giving; it gets us out of scarcity and leads to happiness. Life is beautiful when we're happy and full of love. Love isn't weakness or perverted. Take your time. Step into and be in the present moment as often as you can. It is a great gift to be alive, and the best way to express recognition is to give. That gift can be your time, attention, kindness, and effort, but remember to give to yourself *first* and then expand to others.

Accept your current situation just as it is, not what you think it should be or could be. When we accept the present situation, we open ourselves to options. Accepting isn't condoning. Accept and grow or accept and change. When you refuse to accept, you refuse options and delay the inevitable, possibly even exacerbating a situation that didn't need to get so bad. If we can't change it, then we have to accept it and find a way to work with it. Often, the feeling the situation evokes, is uncomfortable. If we only allow ourselves to ruminate about the discomfort, we miss the chance to transform the discomfort into something else. Great things don't come from comfort zones. Let's not be those people who claim we just want to get by, we just want an ordinary, average life. Why not have a great life? Why not make a significant contribution to those around you, to the community, to the environment?

You have a choice: choose to see clearly, choose to change, choose to be mindful, choose to be kind, choose to be compassionate, choose to be gentle, choose to respond and not react, choose to find your truths, choose to disregard beliefs that don't work anymore, or were never true, choose playfulness, choose light, choose laughter, choose joy, choose happiness, choose being authentic, choose life!

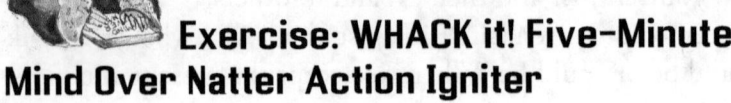

Exercise: WHACK it! Five-Minute Mind Over Natter Action Igniter

Warning: this is a game-changer.

Right now, write now!

We sometimes dream ourselves out of our dreams. We spend too much time thinking about our dreams then doing nothing about them! Doubt sets in and before we know it, the negative inner critics have thwarted us. No more of that! Change starts now. This is a turbo-powered, compact, manifestation exercise. It's CHOOSEday! You are about to be an agent for rapid change in your life right now.

1. Take five minutes. Time yourself. Whatever you've been wanting to do and haven't, there is something you can do in the next five minutes to shift closer to that desire. Write it down in your journal and please put the date next to this entry. Let me know how swiftly the change came for you. Contact me on social media or through my website www.tovekane.com

2. Use this hashtag #tovekanewhackit

3. You don't have to buy anything or sign up for anything. Your dreams are tantalisingly close. Staying stuck feels horrible. Doing something feels incredible. What's your self-limiting doomsday metaphor? Are you deep in a well? Stuck in a rut? Hands tied behind your back? Blindfolded? On a runaway train? Here's the thing: forget about that stuff for five minutes. Take control right now. You have immense power at your fingertips. Before resistance stops you, let me say this—**don't think, just**

DO. Have fun. Choose something that matters to you. If you need any idea starters, try these:

a) Want to go on holiday? Search flights. You have five minutes - go for it.

b) Want to meet someone you could love? Contact your friends and tell them you're ready for their introductions (if it's late at night, no worries, research a dating site in your area). If you don't like dating sites, spend the next five minutes writing down the qualities of your ideal partner. You have five minutes - go for it.

c) Want to get fit? Great. Timer on, right now, this very second, move your body. Do anything: squats, windmills, lunges, jumping jacks, downward dog, plank, step on the spot, dance. If you're seated, clap your hands above your head, do shoulder raises. Move. You have five minutes - go for it.

d) Want to learn a new language? Très bien! Research some conversational phrases or basic greetings. Find a teacher in your area. Learn five new words right now. You have five minutes - go for it.

e) Want more happiness? "Very good, very good yay!" That's how we finish certain Laughter Yoga exercises with that cheerful affirmation. Circle your hands in a big sweeping motion, clap and say, "Very good, very good," and then raise your hands in a wide celebratory "V" above your head and say, "Yay!" Do some silent laughing right now. Open your mouth but don't let any sound out. The pretend laughter could easily bubble over into real laughter and that is an instant experience of happiness, right there. You have five minutes - go for it.

Summary:

W	What you want to be, do, achieve.
H	How it will feel, tap into that feeling now.
A	Action.
C	Clock five minutes.
K	Keep going for the full five minutes and onwards to your goal.

Your five minutes is up, stop the clock!

How was it? The first time I did this exercise I was so exhilarated afterwards I had to go for a run. I searched my heart for one thing I would love. I started the five-minute timer and it was game on! My inner voice said one word: *Greece*.

I was on it. I researched flights to Greece, a place to stay and had time to check my bank balance before the five minutes were up. It's empowering to finally face your inner critics and take action regardless of their negativity. It's even more exciting to listen to the positive ones and follow their prompts. The Five-Minute Mind Over Natter Action Igniter will change your life. Keep doing it and soon you won't even remember your self-limiting beliefs.

I hope to see your breakthroughs. Take a break and enjoy something soothing and when you're ready, there's one more exercise to activate your life.

 **Exercise: What will you CHOOSE for Yourself?**

1. In your journal (which should feel like a good friend by now) draw a pie chart with various life categories. You could distil Mind Over Natter into four quadrants: health, wealth, love and happiness.

There are some suggestions below but this is your chart, design it to suit you. If you want to include a category that relates specifically to love (as in romance or partnership) include that in your chart. You might want categories like: Relationships, Purpose, the Community or the Environment. The options are endless, make it a fun process and don't be surprised if your life starts changing in days, even hours. Sometimes the smallest decision can lead to action which shifts something inside you, opening floodgates of opportunity flowing to you.

I put a heart at the centre of my chart since the heart is my symbol for mindfulness imbued with loving kindness. I try to offer that to each of the categories, even financial.

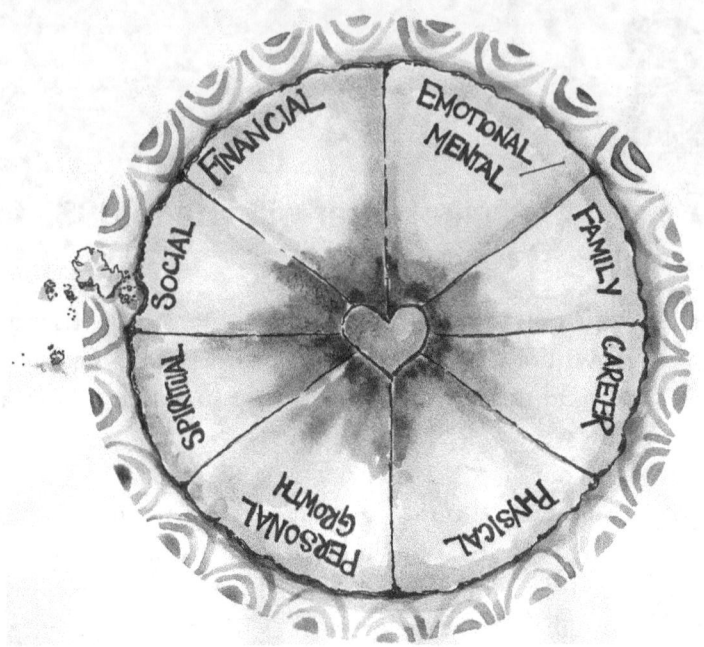

Pie Chart of Life Categories

2. Highlight each section in different colours and perhaps you can use that colour to represent that topic on a vision board or notes in your journal. Order the categories according to your own set of preferences. Maybe your personal growth is most important to you, so place that in the top right. We tend to read pie charts in a clockwise direction. In life, the segments are actually interconnected, there's a lot of cross-over. This is just a graphic way of helping you gain clarity but also showing you that your life is a composite. Your circle becomes a spinning wheel moving you in a positive, expansive direction.

If it helps you to see the list in a linear fashion that's fine, here's how it would look:

Emotional / Mental
Family
Career
Physical
Personal Growth
Spiritual
Social
Financial

3. Next, choose **what** three to five things you'd like to add to your life according to each of your categories. Have fun with this exercise. Would you like to double your income by the end of the year? Express that in your Financial section. If you want to do the couch to 5KM run, add that in your physical category. If you'd like to attract your romantic partner, definitely create that love category and get specific about the qualities of that partner. The clearer our focus, the easier to implement changes. The next phase of the exercise will add another layer of clarity for you: the **when** factor.

4. Now draw four circles representing deadlines for: today, this week, this month, this year.

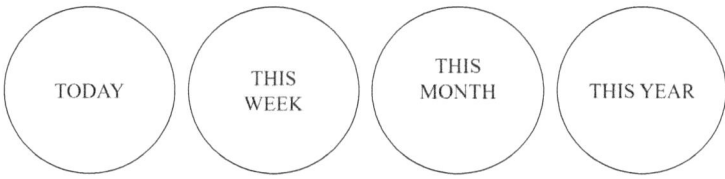

These are all just ideas and dreams until your attach a date. To implement these goals, you have to set **when** deadlines. Your subconscious mind doesn't have a sense of humour. Be clear in your language and speak only in terms of successfully achieving your goals.

Write your goals in a specific time zone: today, this week, this month, this year. You might not be working on all your categories at the same time. In fact, it's easier to break down your tasks into chunks. The best way to achieve a long-term goal is to break it down into smaller, more achievable, short-term goals. These markers along the way add to the momentum and keep you motivated as you draw nearer to achieving it. It's highly motivating to complete a task or reach a goal and this could spur you on to the next or free up some energy for a task elsewhere on the pie chart.

5. ***How does it feel*** to reach your goal? Remember you can't put the cart before the horse. Besides, we've upgraded you remember? You have power and you're driving! Find that feeling of success first, then you attract it into your life. Imagine what it feels like to reach your goal. Now get your Aretha Franklin on in *Freeway of Love* and, "Drop the pedal and go, go, go!" You feel your way to success by taking aligned action and keeping your thoughts locked on success.

Notice, I haven't given any notes on HOW TO achieve your goals. Your intuition will pair with your subconscious mind and the universe will send you signs to take aligned action and that is enough.

Here is the formula:

> Get clear through mindfulness.
>
> Visualise then target what you want.
>
> Stay focused.
>
> Feel good.

Watch for signs.

Take aligned action.

Believe.

Stay grateful.

Give it time.

My complaint mantra used to be *I don't know how*. We know more than we give ourselves credit for, but we have a gap between *knowing* and *doing* and I hope this system will bridge that gap for you. You do know how to do one small thing towards your goal. The rest, you'll learn as you go. Start by visualising, feeling then doing. Be resilient, and have faith.

6. This system is so empowering and effective that you might discover you hit your goals sooner than you expected. When you reach a goal: rest, relax then celebrate. Even the minor victories deserve recognition. Then get going again!

If you feel inspired, add a fifth circle and label it "This life." You might add others that include three, five- or ten-year goals. Nobody could have imagined in 2015 that their five-year goals would have been thwarted by the first ever global lockdown from the Pandemic of Coronavirus Covid-19. My point is: make plans but enjoy the present moment, tomorrow is not promised to us.

Don't get stuck in frustration. Sometimes you're being delayed for good reason. There's always something to learn. Either you're being encouraged to push through, or you're being invited to pause or simply put it down for the time being. Remember to respond and not to automatically react. If you can't figure it out straight away, leave it. We're not used to leaving it, we think we need to be busy with solutions. Stop and take three mindful breaths. First do nothing. Be aware of the pause. Then, move your body. Get out of your headspace. You can even take a nap or go for a stroll or exercise. Play your favourite feel-good tune. Drink some water. Pat your pet. Have a one-minute Laughter Yoga giggle ha ha! Do something kind (that includes you). Then get back to the situation and there will be some clarity on how to shift it. Often, it shifts on its own.

A playful attitude even in the midst of a serious crisis can sometimes help you cope. Situations often resolve themselves. I lean on my primary relationship with God/Source (whatever name you prefer). I suppose you could call it faith. I hand all situations over believing in the right outcome for the highest good, I stay grateful and connected.

I know you've been through a lot, and we both know there'll always be more to overcome. Listen to the encouragement and appreciate the support given to you by your positive inner critics. Don't make a pariah of a negative critic, there's often validity in what they say, but definitely ditch the self-punishment though, it's tedious and counterproductive. Release critics, thoughts and behaviour that no longer serve you. The inner critics are with us for life, work with them not against them.

The rest is up to you! I'm so excited for you. My fingers are flying over the keyboard, and I'm smiling as I write this. I am filled with love, and I delight in knowing you are going to make the changes that will make your life a whole lot happier and healthier. I hope I've given you some inkling as to how to relate to your negative inner critics. Negative inner critics *natter*. Positive inner critics *matter*. Listen to the positive critics encouraging you to go for it!

May you have a dynamic life! May you enjoy the ups and downs and the contrasts as they emerge, knowing you can handle them. May you be happy, healthy, wealthy and loved. May you be peaceful, resourceful, bountiful and joyful.

As I said right at the beginning, and I feel it even more now that we've come this far together, my love and affection are yours, enjoy the journey.

Be kind to yourself and those around you.
All my love
Tové.

YouTube Links for *Mind Over Natter* Meditations

Chapter One Meditation YouTube Link:
https://youtu.be/94nCSLQ0cBM

Chapter Two Meditation YouTube Link:
https://youtu.be/Bso07WFXuHQ

Chapter Three Meditation YouTube Link:
https://youtu.be/3_spt1GS918

Chapter Four Meditation YouTube Link:
https://youtu.be/KlsgtBh9Hfs

Chapter Five Meditation YouTube Link:
https://youtu.be/oGAHLahGsz8

Chapter Six Meditation YouTube Link:
https://youtu.be/mC-2RMsY7yA

ABOUT TOVÉ KANE

Tové Kane is a Professional Keynote Speaker, MC, Voice Artist, Laughter Yoga Leader and Mindfulness Author and Teacher. She is an award-winning Broadcasting Professional. With a background in theatre, training, live radio and television, Tové teaches programmes and courses that boost confidence and proficiency in all facets of Business Communication and Presentation Skills. Through her positive reinforcement and focused workshops, Tové uses the art of mindfulness, combined with her skills as a Laughter Yoga Leader, to guide people through techniques for relaxation, meditation and visualisation to enhance creativity and self-confidence whilst reducing the negative effects of stress. Tové has written for radio, film and television. She is also a photographer, film maker and singer, with numerous commercial songs receiving radio airplay. Tové teaches and presents online and in person. Tové travels extensively. She loves to cook, SCUBA dive, ride motorbikes and horses plus she loves most sport, music, dance and fitness. She is a YouTube Content Creator and is constantly finding ways to bring a smile and healing to her life and those around her. She cares about the environment and has a soft-spot for animals. Stay in touch with Tové on social media and on her website.

https://www.tovekane.com

Enjoyed the book? Now take the next step in the *Mind Over Natter* Online Course.

"Tové's book is worthy, smart, and exactly what our world needs right now."
- Felicity Fox.

Videos, exercises, online interaction—plus, dive deeper into overcoming those negative inner critics, so you can start living your dream life!

Email: info@tovekane.com

BIBLIOGRAPHY

Introduction—What Does Mind Over Natter mean?

1. Langer, Ellen J. Professor. "25th Anniversary Edition, Mindfulness," Da Capo Press, 1989, 2014 xiii

2. Langer, Ellen J. Professor. "25th Anniversary Edition, Mindfulness," Da Capo Press 1989, 2014 116

Chapter Two
Mindfulness—What Is it, and Can I Learn How to Practise It Now?

1. Hanh, Thich Nhat. "The Art of Living, "Penguin Random House, 2017, 55

2. Kabat-Zinn, John, PhD. "Falling Awake," Hachette Books, 2018, ix

3. Hanh, Thich Nhat. "Living Buddha, Living Christ,"Ebury Publishing, 1996, 14,15

4. Fargo, Sean. "Mindfulness Mediation for Beginners," eBook

Chapter Three
Mindlessness—My Life's a Mess. What Can I Do about It?

1. Brown, Brené. PhD. "The Gifts of Imperfection," Hazelden Publishing, 2010, 102

2. Forleo, Marie. "Everything is Figureoutable," Penguin Random House 2019, p12

Chapter Four
Look Who's Talking (and Who's Listening)

1. Singer, Michael A. "The Untethered Soul: The Journey Beyond Yourself," New Harbinger Publication, 2007, 10

2. Brach, Tara, PhD. "Radical Acceptance," Random House, 2003,186

Chapter Five
Selfie Time—Am I Really Not Good Enough?

1. Agam Bansal, Chandan Garg, Abhijith Pakhare, and Samiksha Gupta
Selfies: A boon or bane?
https://www.ncbi.nlm.nih.gov/pmc/articles/PMC6131996/
Accessed 13 April 2020

2. Crocker, Jennifer PhD. Psychologist University of Michigan
   Self-esteem that's based on external sources has mental health consequences
   https://www.apa.org/monitor/dec02/selfesteem
   Accessed 13 April 2020

Chapter Six
Resilience—How Do I Bounce Back?

1. Hicks, Esther and Jerry, "The Vortex" Hay House 2009, 8
2. Hanson, Rick PhD. "Hardwiring Happiness," Penguin Random House, 2013, 20

Chapter Seven
Go for it!

1. Cameron, Julia. "The Artist's Way," Pan Macmillan, 1994, 2016, 11
2. Cameron, Julia. "The Artist's Way," Pan Macmillan, 1994, 2016, 11
3. Shinn, Florence Scovel. "The Game of Life and How to Play it," Martino Publishing 1925, 2016, 3

www.ingramcontent.com/pod-product-compliance
Lightning Source LLC
LaVergne TN
LVHW011811060526
838200LV00053B/3732